The Last Neoliberal

Macron and the Origins of France's Political Crisis

Bruno Amable and Stefano Palombarini

Translated by David Broder

VERSO
London • New York

English-language edition first published by Verso 2021
Originally published in French as *L'illusion du bloc bourgeois: Alliances sociales et avenir du modèle français*
© Raisons d'agir éditions 2018
Translation © David Broder 2021
Translation of the Preface and Afterword © David Fernbach 2021

1 3 5 7 9 10 8 6 4 2

Verso
UK: 6 Meard Street, London W1F 0EG
US: 20 Jay Street, Suite 1010, Brooklyn, NY 11201
versobooks.com

Verso is the imprint of New Left Books

ISBN-13: 978-1-78873-357-1
ISBN-13: 978-1-78873-358-8 (US EBK)
ISBN-13: 978-1-78873-359-5 (UK EBK)

British Library Cataloguing in Publication Data
A catalogue record for this book is available from the British Library

Library of Congress Cataloging-in-Publication Data
A catalog record for this book is available from the Library of Congress
Library of Congress Control Number: 2020948696

Typeset in Minion by MJ & N Gavan, Truro, Cornwall
Printed and bound by CPI Group (UK) Ltd, Croydon CR0 4YY

Contents

List of Tables and Figures

Preface

This book analyses political development in France over several decades, in connection with the projects of economic and social transformation that have characterized this period. The reader will thus find in it the crisis of the old governing parties, the victory of Emmanuel Macron in the 2017 presidential election and the wide programme of neoliberal institutional reforms that the new president has been quick to implement, as well as the political reshaping and modification of social alliances.

The French case certainly has marked characteristics of its own, but it also presents features common to a large part of the European continent. It is therefore possible to draw on the analysis offered in these pages to shed light on the economic and political dynamic of other countries, and to diagnose the future prospects of the European project.

First of all, the collapse of the Parti Socialiste (PS) can be interpreted as a symptom of a more general crisis in the governmental experiences of what is called – ever more misleadingly – the European 'reformist left'. Analysis of the rout of the PS shows that, rather than simply a stalemate of the so-called 'social-democratic' project, we are witnessing the final phase of a movement that has seen parties, in principle of the left, implementing neoliberal reforms not only in France, but also in Spain, Italy, Germany, Greece and the Netherlands. All the parties that have made such attempts (respectively the PSOE, the Partito Democratico, the SPD, PASOK, and the PvdA) subsequently suffered defeats of varying magnitude, but identical in substance, to that of the Parti Socialiste.

On the other hand, the emergence of a nationalist or 'identitarian' right wing which, for reasons that vary from country to country, criticizes the present state of European integration or its pursuit as such, characterizes a large part of the continent, represented by the Front National in France. The most striking political phenomenon in

Germany in recent years has been the rise of the AfD, a party initially based on opposition to the euro, but which has gradually evolved to a fairly classical position of the xenophobic far right. In the United Kingdom, the challenge to the European Union, a deeply rooted sentiment here, was fronted by UKIP. In Italy, a similar role was played by the Northern League, whose transformation from a regionalist and federalist movement into a nationalist party was modelled on that of the Front National.

The weakening of the pro-EU right and the decline of the so-called 'reformist left' parties opened the way for new kinds of governmental coalitions aimed at ensuring the viability of the European construction, strongly analogous to the bourgeois bloc united by Emmanuel Macron in France. This is the case with the German 'grand coalition', as well as the de facto alliance between the Partito Democratico and Forza Italia (Silvio Berlusconi's party) that supported Italian governments from 2013 to 2018.

At the origin of these political reshuffles lies the fracture of the social alliances that formed the basis of alternation between the so-called 'governmental' parties of right and left. This fracture, which has destabilized political systems in a large number of European countries, is most often ascribed to a divergence of interests between social groups that see themselves respectively as winners and losers in the process of economic 'globalization'. We find – at least in France – 'winners' and 'losers' both in groups traditionally linked to the right and in those tending to the left, which partly validates the hypothesis that sees internationalization of the economy as the origin of the political changes under way.

Analysis of the French case, however, makes it possible to identify other causal factors, which suggest additional hypotheses for interpreting the dynamic at work on the European continent. Firstly, there are the long-standing tensions between a left that seeks profound changes in economic and social structures as a route out of capitalism, and a left that is seduced by market mechanisms and adheres, at least partly, to neoliberalism. These precede by several decades the relatively weak influence that the Blairite experience of the Third Way had on the Parti Socialiste. The current period marks a further stage in the conflictual relations between tendencies that had hitherto cohabited for better or worse within the same 'social-democratic' political project. The fracture of the left bloc in France was deliberately produced by the action of the 'Second Left', which saw the working-class component of the alliance as an obstacle to the 'modernizing' action that it sought to promote. Similarly, the neoliberal temptation on the right goes back to the origins of this ideological current, whose influence has steadily grown within conservative parties since the crisis of the 1970s. The experiments of radical neoliberal rupture in the 1980s led by Reagan in the United States and Thatcher in the UK subsequently functioned as ideological attractors for a section of the political class, as well as for a fraction of the traditional right-wing electorate, thus contributing to its crisis, whereas another fraction of this right-wing electorate still expects the state to play a 'protective' role, and is opposed to at least some aspects of the neoliberal turn.

The progressive crisis of the traditional political blocs has led several analysts – in France as elsewhere – to view the right–left divide, which for so long structured the political landscape, as gradually weakening, if not disappearing altogether. In their view, it is being replaced by a new cleavage between 'Europeanists' and 'nationalists' or, in a different but complementary version, between 'managers' concerned with budgetary balances and factors that facilitate long-term economic development, and 'populists' whose sole objective is directly connected with immediate electoral expectations. Some people have even sought to tackle this divide with the fetish opposition dear to some political scientists between 'cultural' authoritarianism and liberalism. It is at least the merit of the Macron experience to have dispelled these illusions of libertarian neoliberalism by showing to what extent a radical neoliberal transformation of society can or even must be based on brutal police repression and significant infringement of civil liberties.

The study of the French dynamic offered in this book allows us both to refine and interrogate the theoretical grid that interprets the political recompositions under way in Europe on the basis of a change in the cleavage structuring political confrontations.

First of all, our analysis emphasizes that the weakening of the right–left cleavage corresponds – contrary to what might be imagined – to an accentuation of the class content of political conflict. The former left-wing bloc, in France as elsewhere, included both a popular component (manual workers, low-grade employees) and a fraction of the middle classes (public-sector employees and executives, intellectual professions, creative trades, and so on). The right-wing bloc was likewise an inter-class alliance that included the other fraction of the middle and upper classes (private-sector executives, liberal professions, sections of the intermediate professions) along with self-employed categories (craftsmen, shopkeepers) and the agricultural world. The axis of political differentiation that seems to be emerging in the present period, on the other hand, clearly separates the well-to-do classes united in the bourgeois bloc around the defence of European integration from the lower classes as a whole, who now perceive the internationalization of the economy and even, increasingly, European unification as direct threats to their living conditions.

Secondly, our analysis of the French case shows that the emergence of this new cleavage is problematic in relation to the conditions that might allow a way out of the political crisis experienced by France and other countries, and the prospects for political change. On the one hand, the bourgeois bloc appears coherent in its support for European integration and neoliberal reforms; but by defending the interests of the privileged classes as a priority, it seems destined to remain a social minority. On the other hand, the political demands that come from the hypothetical alternative bloc, whose aim would be to unite all the popular classes, are strongly contradictory, especially on fundamental issues such as social protection and the wage relationship. On these issues, the popular classes traditionally linked to the right are, at least in part, rather favourable to the 'reforms' that the wage-earning classes clearly oppose.

If the confrontation between political right and left no longer seems an adequate summary of the profile of political conflict in Europe, it would be insufficient and misleading to reduce the political space to the axis dividing Europeanists/managers from nationalists/populists. The political restructurings at work can only be understood in relation to the transformations of the socioeconomic model in Europe.

It is important to stress first of all that the 'pro-Europe' or 'anti-Europe' political strategies that can be observed in various countries are guided by national political concerns. This may explain the paradox that President Macron and the German FDP are divided on the issue of Eurozone reform,[1] even though they essentially share the same ambition with regard to the society and economic model of their respective countries. The paradox is only apparent. In both cases, it is the same political strategy – to achieve a neoliberal model – that is pursued amid different national constraints. In one case, these constraints make it necessary to oppose a significant reform of the Eurozone, perceived as involving a transfer of resources from Germany to other countries, which would weaken the social base necessary for the continuation of the neoliberal transition in Germany. In the other case, in France, reform of the Eurozone is indispensable both for 'economic' reasons – the incompleteness of monetary unification without fiscal federalism; the lack of space for a counter-cyclical macroeconomic policy, which becomes all the more necessary as the labour market has been liberalized and automatic stabilizers have been weakened – and for 'political' reasons, since part of the social bloc supporting Macron only supports the neoliberal transition insofar as it promotes European integration.

An oversimplified view of the structuring of political conflict must therefore be rejected; in particular, because analysis of the French dynamic, which is comparable here to that of Italy, Spain and Germany as well, indicates the diversity of programmes bearing on institutions so fundamental to socioeconomic organization as the wage relationship, international integration and social protection. This observation encourages us to analyse the political recompositions under way on the basis not of the old right–left divide or of a new Europe/nation divide, but of the models of capitalism on which the various projects are based.

Reduced to ideal types, analysis of the French dynamic thus leads to the identification of three main political projects, each of which is guided by a specific vision of overall socioeconomic organization (see Table 0.1).

---

1 Macron declared in the run-up to the German elections of autumn 2017 that if the FDP were to form a coalition with the CDU/CSU, he would be finished.

Table 0.1 Three socioeconomic models

	Neoliberal	*Socialist-ecological*	*'Illiberal'-identitarian*
Wage relationship	Subjection of labour to the interests of capital. Little or no employment protection; individualization, no recognition of the collective interests of employees.	Recognition of the asymmetry of power between employees and employers; employment protection and rules limiting low wages and inequalities; recognized role of trade unions.	No real consideration of the collective interests of employees. Search for an unlikely middle way between individualization without protection and collective protection.
Social protection	Minimal social protection (safety net) and individual private insurance.	Collective protection and benefits independent of contributions.	Protection differentiated according to nationality/identity: minimum for non-nationals.
Production	Privatization of public services. Competitive but practical ideology and policies in favour of private interests and large firms.	Re-nationalization/communalization of privatized public services. Consumer protection against anti-competitive practices of large firms.	'Free competition' demanded within the national framework. Protection of small and national producers.
Finance	Expansion of the finance sector. Financial logic applied to all economic policy decisions.	Supervision of the finance sector and limitation of its influence on economic decisions.	Protection against internationalized finance, at least in words.
Education	Privatized, competitive and elitist system.	Public system with egalitarian ambition.	Tolerance of a private/faith-based system. No egalitarian ambition.
Environment	Outcome left to market mechanisms and private initiative, possibly with state assistance.	Recognition of the ecological emergency and planning to exit the current system based on non-renewable energy.	Active disinterest or even denial of the existence of a problem.

Table 0.1 Continued

	Neoliberal	Socialist-ecological	'Illiberal'-identitarian
European integration	Key project, instrument for implementation of the neoliberal model.	Tensions between the aspirations for a 'different Europe' and acknowledgement that the EU is a vector for the neoliberal transformation of socioeconomic models.	Seen as a problem although some economic policy orientations are compatible with the EU.
Migration	Strictly conditional on the needs expressed by capital.	Contradiction between the egalitarian/ universalist ideal and the fears expressed by the popular part of the social bloc (wages, living conditions, etc.).	Limited to a minimum or even combated.
Democracy / civil liberties	Mistrust of democratic processes; constitutionalization of economic policy; use of brute force if necessary.	Radical democracy.	Delegation of decision to the leader; frequent use of brute repression.
Social bloc	Bourgeois bloc centred on the upper classes (capital) and educated upper-middle classes.	Left bloc in decay. Various possible recompositions according to position towards 'Europe': regaining the lost popular classes or focusing on the intellectual petty bourgeoisie.	Recomposition/ expansion of the right-wing bloc centred on its popular fraction (independents).

On the basis of these three models, which structure the institutional reform projects present in the programmes of all the main French parties and movements, we can understand the difficulty of forming a majority compromise that would provide a real solution to the political crisis we analyse in this book. Each of the three projects actually corresponds to a minority social alliance, while a compromise between two of the three seems hard to envisage. Thus Macron governs France with the support of the bourgeois bloc (a social minority). Against him, the constitution of a hypothetical anti-bourgeois front, which would bring together all the popular classes, faces major contradictions in expectations regarding the wage relationship, social protection, the education system and the environmental question, not to mention migration and civil liberties. At the same time, an expansion of the electorate for the bourgeois bloc, which essentially means the Front National, would come up against the obstacle of opposing attitudes on the European question; and an expansion to the 'left' seems impossible given the content of the reforms that are central to Macron's project.

The three-way polarization that the internationalization of the economy has effected on a political landscape previously structured by the right–left divide – though this is far from having disappeared – is not only characteristic of France: similar features can be found in Italy, Spain, the United Kingdom and Germany. This leads us to conclude that the crisis of political representation, which is in danger of degenerating into a crisis of democracy, is likely to become more pronounced on the European continent.

Of course, a possible reform of European institutions, or a major crisis of the EU and the single currency, would bring about a change in the future dynamics. But a decisive role will also be played by institutional changes within each country; for a complete transition to the neoliberal model, which is on the agenda not only for Macron but also for other European governments, would profoundly alter the content of social expectations, the political definition and weight of socioeconomic groups, and thus the profile of possible social alliances. The political and social conflict currently being played out in France, and more widely in Europe, is therefore of paramount importance: its outcome, which is certainly hard to predict, will not only deeply mark the organization of continental capitalism, but also draw a new and lasting frontier between the dominant classes that participate in the ruling bloc, and the dominated classes whose interests are sacrificed by government action.

Introduction

French politics is undergoing profound transformations. Polls at the start of the 2017 presidential campaign gave strong ratings for both independent candidates Emmanuel Macron and Jean-Luc Mélenchon and to a party often considered 'anti-systemic', the Front National. The political forces that led the governments of the Fifth Republic had clearly been weakened – outgoing Socialist president François Hollande decided against even running for a second term.

This fragmentation of the 'political supply' went hand-in-hand with the rising number of topics on which the presidential candidates' programmes differed. France's participation in the European project, its integration into the global economy, labour law, social protection and pension financing, were but so many fields where past compromises were put back into question – with the candidates' plans diverging on each. Political conflict no longer had to do only with the 'ordinary' instruments of economic policy – such as public spending, fiscal policy, and the minimum wage – but also directly concerned the structuring institutions of French capitalism. Some strategies aimed at defending peculiarly French institutions, whereas others proposed a radical transformation of them in accordance with neoliberal principles.

Yet the political crisis and the conflict over institutions are linked – indeed, in two distinct ways: firstly, because the bid to align French capitalism to neoliberal canons, as notably advanced by the Parti Socialiste over the last thirty years, was itself one of the causes of the political crisis; but also because, through the rupturing of old social coalitions, the political crisis itself encourages political decision-makers to resort to certain institutional changes in order to ease the emergence of hitherto-unknown alliances.

At the start of the 1980s, the political battle was built on the opposition between two social blocs whose contours were relatively clear-cut, and which together represented the vast majority of French society.

The left-wing bloc rallied the majority of low-skilled wage-earners and public employees; the right-wing bloc was based on intermediate professionals, private-sector managers and the self-employed, as well as agricultural France. The political evolution that has been under way across these last three decades coincides with the gradual disaggregation of these two social alliances. We may note that, in the first round of the 1981 presidential election, the candidates of the left-wing bloc (François Mitterrand and Georges Marchais) and the right-wing bloc (Valéry Giscard d'Estaing and Jacques Chirac) together amassed some 87.5 per cent of the votes (over 91 per cent if the Green candidate is included); at the time of the 2017 presidential election, the total percentage belonging to the traditional left and right was below 40 per cent.

It would be mistaken to imagine that we are today seeing some sudden sea-change in the French political landscape: rather, we are living through the terminal phase of a long-term dynamic which started over thirty years ago. Even back in 2002, when Jean-Marie Le Pen reached the second round of the presidential election, this signalled a major political crisis. Only if we drew a very superficial analysis of the political situation of that time could we say that the Socialist candidate's elimination in the first round was owed mainly to the fragmented array of candidates on the left. After all, even 'the parties of government' taken as a whole – whether from right, centre or left – together gathered only 60 per cent of the vote. The 2005 referendum on the European Constitutional Treaty – which produced a 'No' vote, against the recommendations of the vast majority of elected officials – moreover shows that the great split between the expectations emanating from French society and their representation in the political sphere has now been underway for some time.

The unusual context surrounding the 2017 presidential election, which escaped the two-party polarization that had hitherto characterized the Fifth Republic, should thus be understood as a product of a political crisis. It is defined by the absence of a dominant social bloc, which is to say, a combination of social groups whose expectations are sufficiently satisfied by the public policies pursued by the ruling coalition that they will give it their political support. In seeking to explain the dynamic that has led to this situation, this book starts out from an analysis of the social base of the successive ruling coalitions, and of the tensions they have suffered as a result of the policies they have pursued. We will underline both the contradictions that are undermining the right-wing bloc and the factors that have led to the outright explosion of the left-wing bloc.

The French left has been weakened and divided by the end of the 'Trente Glorieuses' (post-war golden age) and the consequent slowing of economic growth. Since the 1980s, the expectations of part of the right-wing electorate – in particular artisans, traders, small business-men and upper-ranking private-sector managers – has been fuelled by the experience of the governments led by Margaret Thatcher in the United Kingdom and Ronald Reagan in the United States. In these groups' view, the only way to revive economic activity is a radical neo-liberal reform, for them particularly identified with tax cuts. But a fraction of the right's social base reliant on wages has, for obvious reasons, been consistently opposed to such a strategy. It instead favours the preservation of certain peculiarities of the French model, especially in the fields of social protection and the labour market.

The French right has still not found any real means of mediation between the contradictory demands coming from its base. Instead, it constantly sways back and forth between its temptation to adopt the harshest neoliberal positions and its stated desire – in some measure inspired by a certain Gaullist tradition – to combat the 'social cleavage'.

The rupture in the left-wing bloc is something rather different – for it is the ultimate result of an ideological and political battle that has been raging in the Parti Socialiste ever since it was founded. As Michel Rocard's so-called 'Second Left' saw things, the social alliance built by Mitterrand in the 1970s, in which the working class bore decisive weight, could not serve as the bedrock for a politics of 'modernizing' French society. The currents led by Rocard and Jacques Delors – heirs to a 'modernist' tradition we will go on to dwell on more closely – were temporarily defeated in the inner-party contest. Yet they did score a decisive success in nailing down European integration as a non-negotiable point in the Socialist programme, to be achieved at whatever cost. The incompatibility between the European integration process and unconditional defence of the French social model hardened the Parti Socialiste's 'reformist' turn. Indeed, once this turn had been embarked upon in the 1980s, it would never be put back into question.

Apparently, at least, the fracture in the left-wing bloc thus took place on the terrain of European integration: the most well-off fraction of this bloc constantly backed a process that the popular part of this alliance increasingly rejected – precisely because this process was the bearer of neoliberal reforms. The depth of the fracture is demonstrated by the violence with which some strategies seek to discredit one part of the old bloc in order to conquer the support of the other part. The working class is described as having retreated into itself, xenophobic and concerned only to defend the advantages it has already acquired. It has, that is, been the victim of an outright campaign of delegitimation, orchestrated partly by intellectuals who claim to be on the left. This theme is dealt with at some length in Chapter 1. In reaction to this, other political strategies have aimed to capture the support of the popular classes that the Parti Socialiste has abandoned, which has in turn accentuated the fracturing of this bloc. Thus, while the workers were treated as retrograde conservatives, the more educated and pro-European fraction of the old left-wing bloc – managers and intermediate professions in the public sector, teaching staff, sociocultural operatives – were themselves caricatured as 'bobos' (*bourgeois bohémiens*). This term – originally coined by the American David Brooks, but much more popular in French than in English – does not have any real sociological significance, but instead offers a crude way of referring to a relatively well-off social group supposedly marked by its cultural openness, but also by the fact that it enjoys certain privileges and rejects income redistribution.

This study shows that the contradiction between the European integration process and the unity of the left-wing bloc is the deliberate outcome of a political strategy. For the European 'constraints' are, in reality, the result of negotiations conducted over the 1980s and 1990s, mostly by the Parti Socialiste, with the quasi-explicit aim of causing trouble for its Communist ally and establishing itself as the only actor capable of guiding the (neoliberal) reform of French capitalism.

Invoking the imperatives of competitiveness and 'economic realism', the Second Left has established its ideological domination over the 'governmental' left. But over the last four decades it has proved far too optimistic with regard to the possibility that, after having broken with a major part of the popular classes, it might go on to find a different electoral majority. Therefore, in order to win power, the Socialists have had to continue to resort to furnishing promises to the traditional left-wing bloc.

The Hollande presidency was not some anomaly in the history of the 'governmental' left. Rather, it was the logical outcome of a course that has been followed since the early 1980s, whose origins – rooted in 'modernist' thinking – in fact date back far earlier. But this path is also a dead-end. The crushing hegemony which the Second Left has won over Socialist leaders, combined with the need to rally the left-wing bloc during electoral campaigns, has produced an unending series of retreats that have eventually proved sufficient to destroy its whole base of political support.

Among those Socialists most attached to the idea that the 'modernization' of French capitalism must be achieved through confrontation with the 'established interests' of the wage-earning classes, it has furthermore become dogma that there are two irreconcilable lefts, and that the so-called 'realistic Left' should openly embrace its convictions and seek its allies in the centre, or even on the right. With his appeal to the 'wise men on all sides', Jacques Delors was the precursor of a strategy. Today, this provides the basis for the position adopted by Emmanuel Macron and, more widely, for the idea that the left–right cleavage is now a matter of the past. The objective here is to bring together an alliance on the basis of European integration, neoliberal reforms and more or less sincere attempts to defend certain parts of the French social model. This is the 'bourgeois bloc'. This project has the merit of explicitly seeking to cohere the political programme of the 'modernization of French capitalism' with an electoral base liable to support it.

The problem is that, even in the hypothetical case where the pro-European fractions from both the left- and right-wing blocs were united into a single whole, the bourgeois bloc would remain a minority in society at large. Only the popular classes' retreat from political exchange and their mass abstention at election time – or the extreme fragmentation of their vote – could allow the bourgeois bloc to impose its own dominance.

A project that can win only on condition that major groups in society disappear from the political process is obviously risky, for it opens up a political space that others will tend to occupy. In reaction to the construction of the bourgeois bloc, a project that has (albeit mostly implicitly) orientated the Parti Socialiste's activity for decades, we have also seen an attempt to form a 'sovereigntist' pole, hostile to the European Union and the euro and in favour of a certain measure of protectionism. This latter's mission is to rally the popular classes as a whole, whether from the left- or right-wing bloc. On the one hand, there are artisans, traders and owners of very small businesses, disappointed by a right considered too timid in its neoliberal reforms; on the other, there are workers and public employees opposed to the neoliberal reforms carried forward by European integration. Thus, in reality, there is a great variety of expectations within the alliance that the Front National proposes to form and represent, especially with regard to labour law and social protections. Unlike the bourgeois bloc, the 'sovereigntist' pole can count on a very broad social base. Yet it is riven by the major contradictions between the different demands of the groups called upon to make up this base – and, for now at least, there is no real plan to mediate them. This explains the Front National's tendency to campaign more on identitarian themes and social mores than on economic proposals.

The French political crisis is not, therefore, rooted in the quarrels in party machines, and still less among individuals. Rather, it expresses the difficulty of forming any new dominant bloc. This difficulty explains why we can see such a proliferation of different strategies, which are far more numerous than they were in the past. The attempts to form new alliances coexist with others seeking to rebuild the traditional blocs. In the pages that follow, we will give a picture of this fragmented landscape and its future prospects. Our belief is that only an analysis of the relations between economic and political dynamics, in a long-term perspective which takes into account at least the last four decades, will allow us to interpret this situation. If we focus too closely on present-day politics, without the benefit of historical distance, it will only appear chaotic, thus thwarting any attempt at theoretical interpretation.

In Chapter 1, we will begin by defining our theoretical approach to the mechanisms for the formation of popular support. We will then review the reasons for the rupture of the social alliances on both left and right – a rupture that is now a relatively old one. Here, we will emphasize that the specificity of the French political crisis lies precisely in the growing exclusion of the popular classes from political exchange. Chapter 2 will be devoted to one of the major actors in this crisis, the Parti Socialiste. Going back in time, we will retrace the origins of its ambition to 'modernize' French capitalism, and underline the links between this ambition and its unbreakable attachment to European integration. Chapter 3 will draw the link between the Parti Socialiste's ideological trajectory and its quest for a renewed social base, consistent with its 'reformist' objectives. This quest has led to the crisis of the left-wing bloc and, in parallel with this, the emergence of a new political project that coincides with the attempt to form the bourgeois bloc. In Chapter 4, we will analyse the recomposition of the political landscape resulting from the crisis of traditional social alliances and the emergence of the bourgeois bloc. This analysis will allow us to identify eight distinct political projects that characterise France's political life. Chapter 5 will propose an analysis of the first part of Emmanuel Macron's presidency. Macron's victory at the 2017 presidential election represented the first electoral success of the bourgeois bloc. The conditions under which this success was possible as well as the difficulties met by the political opposition(s) to the new regime illustrate the ambiguities of the political strategy based on the support of the bourgeois bloc.

CHAPTER 1

The Political Crisis: The Absence of a Dominant Social Bloc

Judging by the French population's growing distrust of political institutions and personnel, there is good reason to believe that the country is experiencing a political crisis. In a 2012 survey for Cevipof,[1] only 31 per cent of respondents said they had confidence in the presidency as an institution, 28 per cent in the National Assembly, and 26 per cent in the government. In this same survey, 85 per cent had reached the conclusion that political officials had 'little or no interest' in their opinion, 52 per cent had no confidence in either left or right to govern the country, and only 12 per cent were 'very' or 'quite' confident in political parties. If we tot up the answers to the question 'What do you feel when politics is being discussed?', we find only 20 per cent of responses are positive: whether expressing interest (13 per cent) hope (6 per cent) or respect (1 per cent). Conversely, negative feelings – distrust (38 per cent), disgust (26 per cent), weariness (12 per cent) and fear (3 per cent) accounted for four-fifths of those surveyed. Of those surveyed, 0 per cent described their feelings in terms of enthusiasm.

The use of the term 'crisis', very widespread in social science literature, spans several different meanings. So it is important to specify the exact meaning this word has in a political economy context. If we want to understand the deep crisis of political representation, we can hardly settle for setting up a counterposition between 'the French' and elected officials. There are differentiated interests even within 'civil society'. We should not expect that any political authority is ever going to represent all of them.

The first step towards a positive analysis of the French crisis is therefore to give up on any notion of the general interest or common

---

1 Cevipof, *Baromètre de la confiance politique*, wave 4, survey conducted in December 2012 (2013).

good, of the 'right' or 'optimal' policy with which everyone could supposedly identify. Public policies instead ought to be analysed as attempts to mediate between differentiated interests – especially socioeconomic interests – which cannot be reduced to any shared perspective. This leaves space for a variety of political strategies to draw different boundaries between those interests they propose to defend or, alternatively, to sacrifice. It is therefore only logical that some part of the electorate will not identify with whatever set of political choices are made. Crisis is a question of extent. If no consensus is possible around *any* particular political strategy, when political support falls to such low levels, the system's stability will come under threat.

We first need to analyse the mechanisms that produce political support, in order to understand what is blocking these mechanisms in today's France. To that end, we first need to reflect on the fact that the evolutions of the economy and of the political go together – and mutually condition one another. Today it is commonplace to analyse the impact that public policy choices have on economic dynamics. But we also need to take account of the opposite movement, running from the economic to the political. The process of economic accumulation is at the origin of a series of – multiple, and partly contradictory – expectations, which each call for political decisions that will protect their interests. Political and electoral support are rooted in the selection and satisfaction of some *part* of these expectations. The modalities of the production and distribution of wealth thus evolve over the course of time – as does the distribution of the power to take the decisions imposed across society as a whole. Indeed, these developments also mutually determine one another. The reproduction of a social structure is possible if the accumulation of wealth and the accumulation of political power, as framed by institutions, mutually reinforce one another (see Figure 1.1).

The economic and the political evolve together, but they respond to different drives. Indeed, the fact that they operate according to heterogeneous logics is at the heart of the reproduction of society, which can thus never be guaranteed in advance. The evolution of the socioeconomic context is always accompanied by transformations in the relations of force. Yet we can speak of a given society being reproduced,

Figure 1.1 The institutions at the heart of political economy

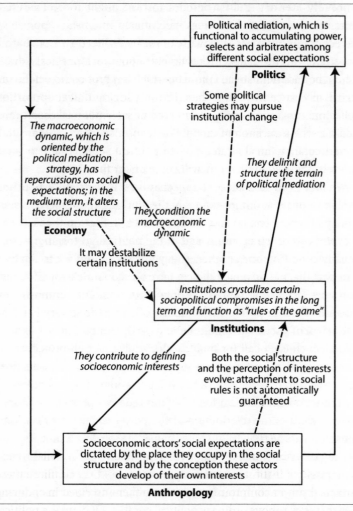

so long as the frontier between the dominant groups (those whose interests are protected by public policy choices) and the dominated ones (those whose interests are sacrificed) is not put into doubt. And yet society's evolutions can lead to crises of varying intensity. Crisis coincides with a challenge to the social order that threatens to throw up obstacles to either political or economic accumulation.

However, frontal opposition to the existing relations of force – the simple refusal to engage in the production and distribution of wealth – is rare. When such resistance does arise, after all, it is heavily punished, whether by unemployment, poverty or exclusion. Even economic-type opposition thus ordinarily makes up part of the sociopolitical sphere: such is the case with social conflicts, which have, of course, not been lacking in France in recent years. In turn, sociopolitical opposition itself comes up against limits: it can even be violently repressed – and, of course, the state has a monopoly on legitimate violence. Here, too, we could point to an abundance of recent examples. Democratic societies are organized in such a manner that opposition to the social order is especially expressed in electoral processes. It is electoral turnout and election results that indicate whether the dominant groups are numerous and powerful enough to confirm the existing relations of force.

Any political strategy must necessarily choose between different social interests. A *social bloc* is made up of the groups protected by a given strategy; it is *dominant* if it is able to validate politically the mediation strategy that provides its own foundation. Thus, the reproduction of a society – that is, the maintenance of a stable boundary between the dominant and dominated interests – depends on the existence of a dominant social bloc. And so, too, does political stability – which is to say, the possibility that the powers-that-be can generate sufficient support to ensure their own viability.

The multiple strategies for political mediation between different interests clash on a terrain defined by *institutions*, which should be understood as the rules of the social game. These rules do not respond to criteria of effectiveness or social justice any more than do the strategies themselves. Institutions are the product of political conflicts; these conflicts result in compromises which are then inscribed in enduring rules that stand above ordinary political conflict. Of course, a political strategy may well set itself the objective of seeking institutional change. But pursuing that goal means reopening a conflict that has temporarily been resolved by way of an institutionalized compromise.

Ordinarily, therefore, the mediation between different interests takes place within an institutional framework which defines constraints that political action must respect if it wants to avoid feeding social conflict. Even so, it may be that no political mediation strategy is able to guarantee the viability of a dominant social bloc within the existing institutional framework. We would term such a situation a *political crisis* – and this is precisely the kind of crisis that is today tearing through France.

The crisis situation directly manifests itself in political instability: the powers-that-be are unable to take any action that will renew the support they need in order to ground their own legitimacy. Instability is thus a consequence of the political crisis, which is itself rooted in the difficulty in constructing a dominant social compromise.

This type of crisis is most simply expressed in election results. Since the end of the 1970s, each French government seeking a fresh mandate at the polls has met with defeat. This is the clearest manifestation of the country's political crisis, which has now been going on for almost forty years. The outgoing majority has, on each occasion, become a minority after the subsequent test at the ballot box; the only exceptions to this rule are owed to the fact that the winners vaunted their opposition to their own camp. Such was the case of Jacques Chirac, elected president in 1995, but in the form of an *outsider* hostile to the outgoing Balladur government; Nicolas Sarkozy did the same in 2007, after having oper-ated as an internal adversary within the Villepin government, standing opposed to the 'immobilism' of the Chirac presidency. Other electoral symptoms of the French political crisis include Jean-Marie Le Pen's progress to the second round of the 2002 presidential election, the victory of the 'No' side – against the recommendations made by all the 'parties of government' – in the 2005 referendum on the European Constitutional Treaty, and indeed the rise over the last three decades of a party considered an 'anti-systemic' force, the Front National. These are well-known events, and they have been widely discussed. In our view, they ought to be seen as *consequences* of a political crisis rooted in the difficulty of forming a dominant social compromise.

In a crisis situation, political actors effectively have no solutions available to them. Within the existing institutional framework, their strategies will be doomed to failure: a *political* failure, corresponding to the impossibility of bringing together a dominant social alliance. This is bound to bring a collapse in the support that political actors need if they are to assert themselves. The political crisis thus has an immediate impact on the institutions themselves. Faced with the impossibility of forming a dominant bloc within a given institutional architecture, institutional change – and the broadened social conflict this change will provoke – will itself be integrated into the various political strategies.

Once again, this change does not at all respond to objectives of economic effectiveness or social justice: it will be adapted to suit the profile of the social bloc that each strategy proposes to bring together. The various political projects thus distinguish themselves in terms of the nature of the institutions they seek to modify and the content of the changes they envisage. This might play out, for instance, in terms of the greater or lesser importance that party programmes accord to rewriting the labour code, to the renegotiation of the European treaties, or indeed to the rules that structure the financial markets. What institutions are most in need of changing, and in what direction should they be changed? To answer these questions, we need to understand the profile of the social alliances that political actors seek to form – and not, necessarily, the economic effectiveness of the strategies they propose. Thus, the conflict over institutional reforms that has characterised France's political landscape for several years is now, in turn, a direct consequence of the political crisis.

THE POPULAR CLASSES, WITHOUT POLITICAL REPRESENTATION

From a theoretical point of view, the political crisis coincides with the difficulty of stably grounding any social bloc capable of sustaining a political strategy. From this perspective, the specific characteristic of the French crisis lies in the more or less complete exclusion of the popular classes *as a whole* from the social alliances on which governmental action (of left or right) has in recent decades sought to base itself.

The *popular* condition corresponds to a subaltern and subordinate position in the division of labour.[2] Even so, it is fundamentally

---

2 Ginzburg uses the term 'subaltern classes', which he draws from Gramsci. Carlo Ginzburg, *The Cheese and the Worms: The Cosmos of a Sixteenth-Century Miller* (Baltimore, MD: Johns Hopkins University Press, 2013).

important for our analysis that we do not consider the popular classes as a homogeneous bloc. As Olivier Schwartz has emphasized

> the notion of the 'popular classes' brings together under a single name a whole array of groups and situations that may in fact be very heterogeneous. Those considered as belonging to the popular classes today can include peasants, blue or white-collar workers, foremen and supervisors, small artisans or traders, the employees of a public company, the young and marginalised, etc. The popular classes' expectations are thus far from identical, for these classes are differentiated by their conditions of existence and their work situations, the social trajectories and experiences most typical of their members, the constraints to which they are subject, the practices and knowledges that they elaborate in order to deal with these constraints, etc. This set of conditions gives rise to cultural traits and ways of life that may mark out far more than just differences of nuance.[3]

As we shall see, in the period that preceded the political crisis, there were fractions of the popular classes present in both the left-wing bloc (blue-collar workers, low-skilled white-collar workers) and the right-wing bloc (artisans, small traders, the underprivileged rural population). However, from the 1980s onwards, these two blocs cracked up and ultimately exploded; since that point any attempt to recompose them has ended in failure. The impossibility of integrating the popular classes into a 'governmental' alliance has even been positively theorized: for the Terra Nova foundation, it is instead now the Front National that 'takes up the position of the party of the popular classes, and it will be difficult to counter this'.[4]

In Terra Nova's view – which expresses a sort of received wisdom among political 'elites' – the FN is an anti-systemic party condemned to opposition. Hence, to delegate the representation of the popular classes to this party amounts to excluding the interests of the weakest

---

3 Olivier Schwartz, 'Peut-on parler des classes populaires?', at laviedesidées.fr (13 September 2011).

4 Terra Nova, 'Gauche: quelle majorité électorale pour 2012?', at tnova.fr (May 2011), p. 15.

Figure 1.2 Vote share for left-wing parties according to socio-professional classification

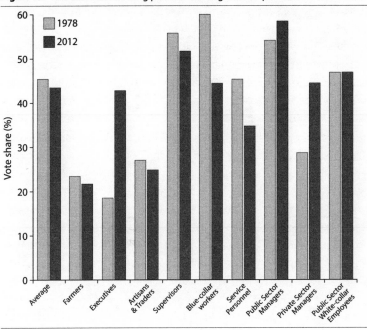

from any political exchange. Indeed, the project of forming a 'bour-geois bloc',[5] as discussed in this book, rests precisely on the political marginalization of the popular classes. In this project, which articulates a new alliance between the middle and upper layers of the old left- and right-wing blocs, the popular classes are excluded.

If the crisis in the representation of the popular classes has become generalized, we will focus more specifically on those social groups who historically sought – and sometimes found – the answer to their expectations within the political left. The left has never represented the popular classes as a whole, but rather a very sizeable part of those classes. To simplify things – without drifting too far from the reality – we could say that the left was long supported by the waged popular

5   In this book, the expression 'bourgeois bloc' refers to a social alliance centred on the educated middle and upper classes. The same expression is sometimes used, for instance in Switzerland, to refer to something else, most often meaning an alliance of right-wing political parties.

Figure 1.3 Vote share for right-wing parties according to socio-professional classification

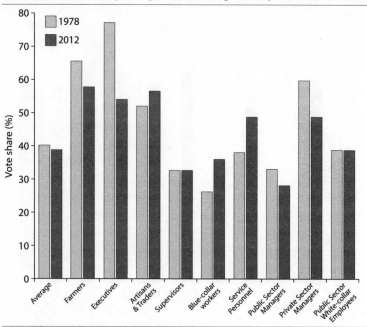

classes, which is to say, those whose relation of subordination was formalized in an employment contract.

Figures 1.2, 1.3 and 1.4 show the votes for the parties of left (including the far left) and right (including the far right), as well as abstention, as distributed by socio-occupational category, according to election polls for the years 1978 and 2012.

The 1978 figures show relatively clearly that the popular vote favoured the left and stood at a distance from the right. Conversely, the study of the 2012 electorate reveals the popular classes' disaffection with the left and rising support for right-wing and far-right parties – but, most importantly of all, their increased levels of abstention. According to INSEE,[6] in 2012 blue-collar workers still represented more than 20 per cent of the active population, and even a slightly greater proportion of the total population if we also include pensioners. If we combine

---

6 INSEE, *France, portrait social*, 2014 edition.

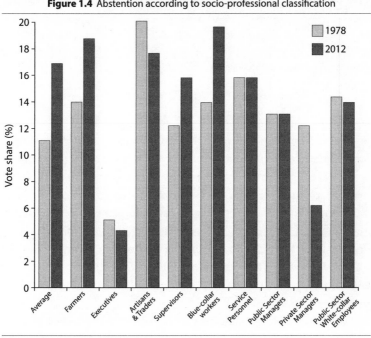

Figure 1.4 Abstention according to socio-professional classification

this percentage with the figure for white-collar workers (whose average salary is lower than their blue-collar counterparts), we arrive at around half of the active population. Since the 1980s, the relationship between these classes and the left has entered into crisis. The historical evolution of the blue-collar vote for Socialist candidates in second-round presidential contests shows that, while there was once a very strong and privileged link between the left and this fraction of the popular classes, over time this bind has weakened to the point of disappearing almost entirely. In 1974, the Socialist candidate François Mitterrand secured more than 68 per cent of the blue-collar vote in the second round, as against 49.2 per cent overall – a 19 per cent gap. But, in each fresh presidential election since then, the difference between the blue-collar vote and the national average decreased: it was 15 per cent in 1981 and 14 per cent in 1988 (each time for Mitterrand), then 10 per cent in 1995 (Lionel Jospin), 8 per cent in 2007 (Ségolène Royal) and 4 per cent in 2012 (François Hollande).

Table 1.1 Presidential election second round votes for the Socialist candidate
Per cent of worker vote (difference from the national average)

1974	1981	1988	1995	2007	2012
+19%	+15%	+14%	+10%	+8%	+4%

Source: Figures based on Sofres post-election surveys.

BLUE-COLLAR WORKERS AND THE LEFT:
THE RHETORIC OF AN INEVITABLE RUPTURE

For Terra Nova,[7] a think tank that exerts strong influence on Parti
Socialiste strategy, the rupture between the left and the popular classes
that it once represented is an inevitable process. In its view, 'the Left's
historic coalition, centred on the working class, is in decline'. Sum-
moned to take over from this coalition is, it seems, a 'new coalition',
'the France of tomorrow'. This latter is portrayed as 'younger, more
diverse, more female, with higher qualifications, more urban and less
Catholic'; above all, this France of tomorrow is culturally progressive
and also supports free-market economics. For this new coalition is
made up of 'outsiders'.

Here, Terra Nova is referring to the distinction between insiders
and outsiders invented by economists in the 1980s and then reworked
by political scientists in the 2000s. In this perspective, the outsiders'
expectations for public action are profoundly different from those of
the insiders. According to this simplistic view of the segmentation
of employment, the outsiders want action to 'break the glass ceiling',
while the insiders want only to protect their own position, to the detriment of outsiders. In this view, these outsiders thus constitute 'the
Left's new "natural" electorate'.[8]

The opposition between insiders and outsiders is taken as the fundamental political cleavage, defining the categories whose employment
status gives them social privileges in opposition to the less protected
layers of society. For Terra Nova, blue-collar workers – or at least those
enjoying permanent contracts – would thus make up part of the privileged group. For the think tank, the crisis in these workers' relationship
with the left is explained by three fundamental factors:

7   Terra Nova, 'Gauche'.
8   Ibid., p. 5.

1. Globalisation: 'The social model promoted by social democracy – the social-market economy, built around the construction of the welfare state – is no longer compatible, as is, with the new globalised world. It must be refounded'.[9] In this perspective, globalization should force the Socialist left not only to change its social base and wave goodbye to the workers, but also to rethink its historic role, which has been largely centred on the construction of the welfare state and the gradual expansion of wage workers' rights. In Terra Nova's portrayal, these same rights earn workers on permanent contracts the title of 'privileged insiders'.

2. The shrinking of the working class and the decline of working-class identity: 'After a century of growth, since the 1970s the working-class population has been contracting rapidly, now representing only 23% of the active population – meaning a 40% collapse in the left's electoral bedrock. This phenomenon, the corollary of the country's deindustri-alisation, is amplified by the numbing of class feeling: only a quarter of blue-collar workers identify with the working class. The explanation for this lies in the internal recomposition of the world of work. The number of unskilled workers has fallen sharply, in favour of skilled and better-paid workers able to make up part of consumer society, and who identify more with the middle classes. Moreover, industrial workers represent only 13% of the active population: two-fifths of workers work in the tertiary sector as drivers and logistics or warehouse staff. These service workers, who work in isolation from each other, no longer benefit from a working-class identity: that is, from the labour collective of the factory, the trade-union tradition and the pride in one's craft.[10]

3. If these two first factors behind the crisis in the relationship between the Socialist left and blue-collar France – as identified by Terra Nova – are indeed inevitable, the third is entirely the workers' own doing. For at the origin of the divorce was a change in values: 'From the 1970s the rupture developed at the cultural level. May '68 drew the political left toward cultural liberalism: sexual freedom, contraception and abor-tion, and the challenge to the traditional family ... this shift on societal

---

9   Ibid., p. 6.
10   Ibid, pp. 6–7.

questions hardened over time, and is today embodied in tolerance, openness to diversity, and a favourable attitude toward immigrants, to Islam, to homosexuality, and to solidarity with the most disadvantaged. In parallel, blue-collar workers have headed in the opposite direction. The decline of the working class – the rise in unemployment, increased precarity, the loss of collective identity and class pride, the difficulties of living in certain neighbourhoods – have given rise to reactions based on retrenchment: against immigrants, against welfare recipients, against the loss of moral values and against the disorders of contemporary society.'[11]

Declining at the social level and holding expectations incompatible with the globalization of the economy, the working class has thus, it seems, retreated into its own cultural niche – displaying its intolerance towards immigration and the societal changes produced by 1968, including liberation from traditional mores. How can the left still represent blue-collar France – and, more importantly, why should it even set out to do so? In Terra Nova's view, 'economic factors are losing their decisive importance to the blue-collar vote'; rather, 'cultural factors, fuelled by the economic crisis and "raised to a hysterical pitch" by the far right' are becoming the preeminent factors in voter choice. This is taken to explain blue-collar workers' swing towards the right, and towards the Front National in particular. 'Nowadays, workers position themselves above all as a function of their cultural values – and these values are deeply anchored to the right.'[12]

We should first note that this analysis is factually incorrect. If it is true that the privileged bind between workers and the left has weakened considerably, almost to the point of disappearance, it is wrong to say that the working-class vote has swung en masse towards the FN and the right: as we indicated above, this electorate has shifted not so much towards the far right as towards abstention. Thus, to take one example, the IPSOS study on the 2015 regional elections confirmed that the Front National is the leading party in blue-collar France (43 per cent

---

11   Ibid., p. 7.
12   Ibid., p. 26.

of those who voted). But we would get a misleading view of the real picture if we overlooked the fact that, according to this same survey, fewer than two in five workers actually turned out to vote. The more accurate representation of the blue-collar vote in the 2015 regional elections would be as follows: abstention 61 per cent, Front National 16 per cent, left-wing lists 13 per cent, right-wing lists 9 per cent. We find similar results – albeit less impressive ones – for the waged popular classes as a whole. In their great mass, these latter took refuge in electoral silence, far fewer of them heading into the FN's embrace. As we go up the social ladder, we see a dual shift: as the percentage for turnout rises, the vote for the Front National falls.[13]

A second consideration concerns the changing values that have supposedly distanced blue-collar workers from the Left. For Terra Nova, 'The higher an individual's qualification levels, the closer they stand to the cultural values of the left' – namely: 'liberal stances on moral questions, tolerance, openness to cultural differences, acceptance of immigration'.[14] In this presentation, adherence to 'left-wing' values rises in tandem with one's level of study. Blue-collar workers and low-skilled workers more generally would thus no longer be left-wing from a cultural point of view – and the left would have to reckon with that fact. Yet a basic assumption is made in the Terra Nova study which it never goes on to discuss: How was this list of *left-wing cultural values* determined, and by whom? We might suppose that the results Terra Nova arrives at – identifying managers and the upper socioeconomic categories as the most left-wing classes from the cultural point of view[15] – would have looked quite different if values like equality or solidarity[16] (absent from the list used) had been included in its characterization of left-wing culture. More generally, the decision to overlook everything to do with what was once called the 'social question' can only distort the portrayal of 'left-wing values' in favour of the expectations of the most (culturally) privileged classes.

13   IPSOS, 'Régionales 2015. Sociologie des électorats et profil des abstentionnistes' (December 2015).

14   Terra Nova, 'Gauche', p. 29.

15   Ibid., p. 27.

16   And not only solidarity with the 'poorest'.

Finally, we could note that this analysis presents the divorce between the left and blue-collar workers as having nothing to do with the public policies that French governments have pursued over the last thirty-five years. Here we have globalization, the transformation of industry, the decline of the working class, and a change in values: but Terra Nova says not one word on policies concerning fiscal policy, social protection or the labour market. Or, when they are mentioned (for instance, with reference to the Mitterrand administration's *tournant de la rigueur* – austerity turn – in 1983), the policies implemented are more or less explicitly considered 'inevitable' consequences of the factors mentioned above (globalization and so on). This is, allegedly, the reason why blue-collar workers' expectations in the field of economic policy have become impossible to satisfy (the social-market economy is no longer compatible with the globalized world, Terra Nova tells us). As a consequence, it is no longer possible to distinguish left from right at the level of economic policies. In this understanding, the only remaining dimension to exploit, if one wants to distinguish oneself politically, is that which regards 'cultural' questions. This reasoning betrays a strictly two-dimensional – economic, and 'cultural' – portrayal of the political space. And this is a portrayal to which contemporary political scientists hold especially dear.

This limited conception of the structuring of the political space allows Terra Nova to characterize the divorce between blue-collar workers and the left as an inevitable process:

> Today it is impossible for the left to try to restore its historic class coalition: the working class is no longer the heart of the Left's vote, it is no longer in step with its values, it can no longer be the driving force behind the formation of an electoral majority on the Left, such as it once was. The Left's desire to build a class strategy around the working class, and the popular classes more generally, would demand that it give up on its own cultural values, which would mean a break from social democracy (p. 13).[17]

---

17   Terra Nova, 'Gauche', p. 13.

The observations we have made raise considerable doubt over Terra Nova's central argument, according to which blue-collar workers have swung to the far right on cultural and identitarian grounds. However, this thesis is the basis of the report's central political conclusion: namely, that blue-collar workers have become the pillar of the Front National's electoral support.

> The FN today defines itself as a 'national' and 'social' party, very much on the Right on cultural questions and on the Left on social and economic ones. It thus very exactly aligns with the values of the blue-collar electorate. For the first time in three decades, there is a political party in step with blue-collar aspirations as a whole. That is why it will be difficult to stop the FN becoming the party of blue-collar workers. And, more generally, the party of the working popular classes: white-collar workers have values close to those of their blue-collar counterparts and will thus be equally susceptible to the FN's siren song.[18]

Thus, the left ought to recompose itself not on the basis of a class logic, but on the basis of values issues:

> The identity of the Left's historic coalition was once found in a class logic: with the 'exploited' workers against the bosses and the representatives of capital, and modestly-off wage-earners, blue and white-collar workers against the managers and the upper-middle classes ... The recomposition that is now underway takes place on the basis of values. It is structured around the relation with the future: that is, investment in the future as against the defence of the present. The new Left has the face of the France of tomorrow: younger, more feminine, more diverse, with better qualifications, more urban. This France of tomorrow, today being built, is united by cultural values: it wants change, it is tolerant, open, solidaristic, optimistic, and on the offensive. The France of tomorrow stands opposed to an electorate that defends the present and the past against change.[19]

---

18   Ibid., pp. 46–7.
19   Ibid., p. 54.

Of course, in this outlook blue-collar workers and the 'working popular classes' ought to be counted among the conservative electorate. They are thus necessarily excluded from the new 'social-democratic' coalition, which will instead bring together outsiders who encounter difficulties in 'entering into society' – namely, 'the young, women, minorities, the unemployed'. The source of their difficulties, according to Terra Nova, lies in the insiders' wish to 'preserve the rights they have acquired'.

Terra Nova recognizes the need for public action – the need to change this regrettable state of affairs by allowing the outsiders to 'overcome the barriers put in their way'. Happily, these unfortunate outsiders will benefit from disinterested support from some of the better-off, 'the most integrated (those with university degrees), who out of their cultural convictions stand in solidarity with these "excluded" citizens'. So, who are these outsiders' enemies?

> An individualist and liberal France that distrusts social solidarity and the role of the state: senior citizens, artisans and traders, farmers, Catholics ... But also, and this is new, the under-threat "insiders": blue- and white-collar workers who fear for their economic status (their permanent contracts) and their social privileges. They want state intervention, but to their own advantage: to protect the rights they have acquired which are now under threat. Here we have the state-as-protector as against the state-as-emancipator, 'protect me' against 'help me succeed'.[20]

This rhetoric adopts the classic reasoning we find in the literature on 'insiders' and 'outsiders', which can be summarized as follows: the 'protections' (labour legislation) which insiders enjoy (unduly so, of course) come at the cost of outsiders' growing precarity. According to this understanding, these latter are demanding nothing more than the abolition of these fetters to labour market competition. Yet when we ask these outsiders what they themselves think, what they want is not so much the dismantling of labour law as access to a non-precarious job.[21]

---

20 Ibid. p. 55.
21 Thus those we might term insiders are relatively more in favour of measures

Workers and the popular classes are now supposed to be culturally bound to the far right; the left, therefore, could not even attempt to respond to their expectations. The corollary of this central thesis is that the left's mission is no longer to advance workers' rights, but should instead consider these the 'established rights' which set up obstacles to change and to the protection of the interests of the weakest categories (outsiders). Any crisis in the left's relationship with the wage-earning popular classes is thus considered unavoidable.

A PLANNED AND DELIBERATE RUPTURE

Nonetheless, it should be repeated that, contrary to what Terra Nova tells us (a discourse analogous to that of a large part of the media, or else the same but turned inside-out) this crisis only very marginally translates into a vote for the Front National. Of much greater significance is the reaction that Patrick Lehingue, adopting the classification of the economist Albert Otto Hirschman, characterizes in terms of exit:[22] the rise of abstention, dating back to the second half of the 1980s. Among workers, abstention levels reached 59 per cent in the 2012 presidential election, 65 per cent in the 2014 European elections and – as we have seen – 61 per cent in the 2015 regional elections.[23] We shall note in passing that the strategy of exit concerns not only blue-collar workers and public-sector employees (who display similar levels of abstention) but also – in even greater measure – the unemployed. For all these categories, turnout has fallen to well under half, and at least from this point of view we find no trace of the insider–outsider cleavage Terra Nova's analysis takes as its starting point.

As Lehingue stresses, the massive crisis in the political representation of the popular classes is expressed not only in voting, but also

---

to liberalize the labour market, such as the *contrat unique*, whereas this proposal (which appeared in Nicolas Sarkozy's 2007 programme, receiving sporadic positive references from PS officials like Manuel Valls) is more widely rejected among social groups we might term outsiders. See Bruno Amable, 'Who Wants the Contrat de Travail Unique? Social Support for Labor Market Flexibilization in France', *Industrial Relations* 53: 4 (2014), pp. 636–62.

22   Patrick Lehingue, 'Les classes populaires et la démocratie représentative en France: *exit, voice* ou *loyalty*?', *Savoir/Agir* 31 (2015), pp. 25–34.

23   Ipsos, 'Regionales 2015'.

directly, in the profile of elected representatives. In the 2012 parliamentary elections, only twelve former workers or public employees were elected to the National Assembly; in 1945, there had been ninety-eight of them. If these categories had been represented proportionately they would have had some 290 MPs (166 white-collar workers, 124 blue-collar). Similarly, in 2012, of the 260 *communes* of over 30,000 inhabitants, the mayors of just six (2.4 per cent) were former workers or public employees; in 1983, there had been seventy-eight of them.[24]

For the fatalistic Terra Nova, this development in the relationship between workers and the left is the product of objective factors (globalization, the transformations of industry) and working-class values evolving towards retrograde prejudices. But a more serious analysis must also take into account the decline of their organizations, the precaritization and fragmentation of their universe, the downgrading of their economic and symbolic positions, and, above all, the deliberate public policy choices left-wing governments have made since the 1980s.

The left's split with the popular classes is thus, at least in part, the result of a political project that has set out to discredit workers. According to Gérard Mauger,[25] and indeed Julian Mischi[26] – who is more particularly interested in the trajectory of the Parti Communiste Français (PCF) – the discrediting of workers has taken place at three levels: the economic, the political and the symbolic. This process has spanned the three generations identified by Gérard Noiriel.[27] The first was the 'heroic generation' that took part in the struggles of the Front Populaire and the Resistance. It was followed by the 'modernization generation', which benefited from the extension of protections by the welfare state, the rise in purchasing power, and so on. It was followed in turn by the 'crisis' generation, which has endured the consequences of mass unemployment and the extension of precarity.

---

24   Lehingue, 'Les classes populaires'.

25   Gérard Mauger, 'Sur la participation des classes populaires aux nouveaux "jeux électoraux"', *Savoir/Agir* 2007, 1, pp. 49–58.

26   Julian Mischi, 'Au nom des ouvriers. Quelle représentation politique des classes populaires?', *Mediapart*, 16 March 2012.

27   Gérard Noiriel, *Les Ouvriers dans la société française, xixe-xxe siècle* (Paris: Seuil, 1986).

Counter to Terra Nova, Mauger and Mischi consider the precaritization of workers' employment first of all as the result of a political strategy, and not as an inevitable phenomenon. The economic changes in the working-class condition – tertiarization, precaritization, the forms of blackmail linked to the spread of mass unemployment – have their political counterpart, according to Mauger, in

> the successive disappointments brought by the successive 'turns to the centre' by the 'governmental' Left. [This disillusionment] takes place amidst the confusion engendered by the ever more interchangeable character of [parties'] programmes, in the collapse and discrediting of 'actually-existing socialism', in the symbolic devaluation of Marxism and, by extension, of critical thinking, in the desertion of the *grands ensembles* ['big high-rise housing estates'] which have become 'sensitive neighbourhoods' by militants often closer to the 'établi' [a militant who 'industrializes', or takes a working-class job in order to organize the workplace] than to the 'marginal', in the internal divisions between 'discredited' (for different reasons) pretenders for the representation of the 'cause of the people' in the absence of credible alternatives, etc.[28]

Mischi identifies the Parti Communiste's particular responsibility in this political dimension of the discrediting of workers:

> The distancing of the popular classes from the PCF … also results from a political strategy which gradually leaves behind working-class militants in favour of the 'new social layers', notably engineers, technicians and managers. The Communist officials who emerged in the *départements* in the late 1970s were, for sure, very often of working-class origin; but they had worked on the shopfloor to an increasingly lesser degree, before rapidly rising to the status of full-time officials. The number of full-time officials rose throughout the 1970s, surpassing one-thousand at the end of that decade. Most importantly, there was an increase in the share of elected representatives who were full-timers, and of those drawing their salaries from the local

---

28   Mauger, 'Sur la participation des classes populaires', pp. 49–58.

administrations run by the PCF. The relationship with working-class populations passed ever more by way of administrators, elected officials and functionaries, and increasingly less by way of militants. The maintenance of Communist municipalities became a centrally important question and the possession of educational resources and 'administrative competences' gradually came to appear advantageous for being active in the PCF and rising up its internal hierarchy.[29]

But there is another, fundamental dimension to the strategy of discrediting the working-class condition. This is the symbolic dimension. 'This is exercised in multiple ways', writes Mauger:

> not only through racism and/or 'class racism' (associated with the figure of the '*beauf*' [the redneck or 'gammon']), but also through the disorientation efforts which have endeavoured, under the banner of modernisation, to discredit the old words ('worker', 'working class', 'exploitation', 'class struggle', etc.) in the political field, the media field but also in the intellectual field, and replaced them with smokescreens: the OS [assembly-line worker] metamorphoses into the 'operative', the factory into the 'enterprise', the strike into the 'social movement', layoffs into 'social plans', the foreman into the 'supervisor', the boss into the 'entrepreneur', etc. The loss of the 'words of the clan' does not only produce a discursive disarray but also denies value to a past which is now supposed to have no future.[30]

Here, too, the Parti Communiste has its share of responsibility. 'At the end of the 1970s', Mischi writes,

> especially in the framework of the *Cahiers de la misère* campaign, the PCF tended to present itself as a spokesman for 'the poor'. Voiced by the full-timers furthest from the world of industry, this discourse abandoned the notion of 'working class'. It was often out of step with workers, who no longer recognised themselves in the devaluing image

---

29   Mischi, 'Au nom des ouvriers'.
30   Mauger, 'Sur la participation des classes populaires'.

which was attached to them. In turning toward the 'excluded', the Communists eventually turned themselves into spokesmen of categories in need of aid and no longer – as in the workers' case – of mobilisation and access to political power.[31]

The symbolic delegitimation of working-class France was, in reality, a process involving multiple actors. The Terra Nova report that we have cited has no real interest as a positive analysis of the rupture between the 'governmental' left and the popular classes. Indeed, it is merely caricatural in its complete omission of the role that the policies effected by left-wing governments played in this rupture.

Nonetheless, through its aggression towards the working-class universe and its values, this report very well illustrates the *deliberate* character of the Socialists' rupture with working-class France. This latter has been weakened at the economic level, and is widely underrepresented politically – but it also had to be delegitimized symbolically.

THE RUPTURING OF OLD ALLIANCES — SOURCE OF THE POPULAR CLASSES' CRISIS OF REPRESENTATION

If we want to grasp the crisis of representation in France, we need to analyse the obstacles that the attempts to form a dominant social bloc have encountered. These obstacles are in large part linked to the responses that public decision-makers have given to the popular classes' expectations in recent decades.

To understand this political crisis we should not, therefore, start out from supposedly exogenous and inevitable phenomena like globalization and industrial or cultural shifts, but rather from an analysis of governmental strategies. Indeed, this crisis largely coincides with – and is explained by – the exclusion of the popular classes from political exchange. This plays out both at the level of attempts to secure their electoral support and the defence of their economic interests.

---

31   Mischi, 'Au nom des ouvriers'.

The two social blocs

For several decades in French political history, two social blocs corresponding to two different political coalitions alternated in power.[32] The sociopolitical landscape of the France of the late 1970s and early 1980s was relatively simple compared to today's: there were two distinct social alliances with differentiated expectations and easily identifiable political organizations.

The left-wing bloc, which rallied the majority of public-sector employees and the blue-collar working class, was represented by the Parti Socialiste and the other left-wing parties, in particular the Parti Communiste. The two parts of the left, which had been opposed to one another during the Fourth Republic, built an alliance, the Union de la Gauche, which despite its fragmentation in 1977 still constituted a reference point for the left-wing electorate into the early 1980s. The expectations which structured the left-wing bloc pointed in the direction of greater state intervention in the economy, an extension of workers' rights and social protections, and increased living standards, especially for those on the lowest wages.

The right-wing bloc was organized around managers and intermediate professionals in the private sector, the liberal professions, the self-employed and artisans, a large part of agricultural France, and practising Catholics.[33] It was politically represented by the Gaullist party and its liberal allies. This right-wing bloc called for state intervention by way of an industrial strategy that would protect national interests, meaning French businesses. This bloc was opposed to more nationalizations, which by contrast constituted an essential point in the left's programme for government.

The right-wing bloc also differentiated itself from the left-wing alliance in terms of the state's social and redistributive actions: the left-wing alliance wanted to reduce income disparity by increasing

---

32   It could be argued that this division into two blocs in fact came after 1958 and the birth of the Fifth Republic, but that question is beyond the scope of this work.

33   We can also notice an age bias in the separation between the two blocs: the oldest tend, other things being equal, to join the right-wing bloc. Support for the right among seniors has not fallen over succeeding decades.

taxes, whereas the right-wing alliance preferred tax cuts, even if this meant that inequalities widened. Within this framework, private-sector employees played a pivotal role, because the majority could swing to either bloc – and thus ensure its electoral victory – depending on the economic conjuncture and the parties' given electoral programmes.

This situation – which was politically regulated, because its axes were based upon stabilized alliances – began to mutate in the early 1980s. This shift was owed to internal contradictions that developed within each of the two blocs.

The right-wing bloc's difficulties

We will go on to review in some depth the main contradiction which first fissured and then exploded the left-wing bloc – a contradiction directly connected to European integration. But major contradictions also emerged within the other bloc. On the right, the political mediation founded on a state-guided search for competitiveness faced challenge in the 1980s – indeed increasingly so from the part of the alliance most characterized by the popular classes: artisans, traders and owners of very small businesses.

This challenge resulted from the interpenetration of two factors. On the one hand, the slowdown in growth made the relatively high level of employee protections more punitive for these groups, which were far from the most productive or competitive part of the French economy. This was married to the relatively high tax levels which necessarily accompanied the role the state played in the post-war French model of capitalism. On the other hand, the examples of Margaret Thatcher and Ronald Reagan – who were both highly successful electorally – showed that *another right was possible*. These Anglophone examples became models of reference for the Front National of this era – posing as a competitor to the republican right – but also the source of a major cleavage within the 'governmental' right itself.

Neoliberal policies are thus at the heart of the problems affecting not only (as we shall see) the left-wing bloc, but also the right-wing bloc. The right-wing alliance around the RPR-UDF/UMP coalition was three times in power for two-year spells (1986–88, 1993–95 and 1995–97), and then between 2002 and 2012. For its part, the Chirac government in 1986 drew a great deal of inspiration from the 'conservative revolution' that had taken place in the United Kingdom and the United States. It reached power with the stated ambition of radically changing the structures of the French economy. The reform programme was centred on privatizations – that is, a radical reversal of the economic policy conducted by the left-wing alliance in 1981 – and, in less marked fashion, a flexibilization of the labour market. A vast privatization programme was launched, and the obligation on businesses to obtain administrative authorization for lay-offs was abolished. This had major consequences in terms of the opportunity which companies were given to deploy restructuring policies – with inevitable repercussions in terms of job cuts.

This neoliberal orientation sparked problems even within the right's own social base, driving an opposition between groups demanding greater labour market flexibility (artisans, traders, the self-employed) and those who felt threatened by it (particularly wage-earners in the private sector). The neoliberal flexibilization of the labour market – and, to a lesser extent, some privatizations – thus clashed with the needs of some groups within the bloc in terms of economic security, public services and redistribution.

Jacques Chirac's venture in 1986 was more a matter of aligning his agenda to the expectations of *part* of his social base – favouring a radical neoliberal transformation – than of mediating between the various expectations within the right-wing alliance.

The failure of the 1986–88 experience would have a lasting impact on the political strategies the right pursued. Leading right-wing politicians took on board the fact that the strong demand for liberalization and the flexibilization of the labour market, coming from part of their electorate, was difficult to reconcile with the demands for security expressed by private-sector employees. This fundamental contradiction explains the caution shown in subsequent labour-market reforms, up until Nicolas Sarkozy's presidency. The only serious attempts to flexibilize the labour market were always made around the margins, targeted at specific groups of the active population and not at its very core.[34] Ironically, the most significant neoliberal reform of labour relations was undertaken under the presidency of the Socialist François Hollande.

In 1993–95, Édouard Balladur's government abstained from making any major changes to the labour market. It concentrated rather more on pursuing a programme of privatizations, with the objective of forming hard cores of stable shareholders as selected by the Finance Ministry.

A first important reform to reduce social protection concerned private-sector pensions – a risky move, given the composition of the right's social base, which was heavily reliant on 'seniors'. Although the reform passed without provoking any significant reaction from the unions, it added to the difficulties Édouard Balladur faced in his competition with Jacques Chirac for the leadership of the right. Indeed, Chirac could seize the opportunity to mark himself apart from the neoliberal orientation by proposing a mediation between the diverging demands of the right-wing bloc, very different from Balladur's own.

Hence, in the 1995 presidential contest, Chirac beat Balladur in the first round, and then won the run-off against Lionel Jospin by adopting an almost centre-left position. He criticized the Balladur government's lack of reaction faced with growing inequalities (as foregrounded by the theme of the 'social fracture') and promised a policy to kick-start growth that would increase purchasing power ('The payslip is not the enemy of employment', as he put it). Chirac's proposals allowed him to unite the right-wing bloc. Yet, once elected, Chirac and his prime minister Alain Juppé embarked on a more classic neoliberal policy than the calls to overcome the 'social cleavage' would have suggested.

An important turning point here was the failure of the 1995 pensions reform. Juppé did show some caution, in that he targeted a group that largely identified with the left-wing bloc – civil servants and the employees of public companies, with their special retirement plans. This reform represented a bid to align these special pension plans with

---

34 Such attempts to make adjustments around the edges included De Villepin's CPE (*Contrat première embauche*: First Job Contract) for those under twenty-six and the CNE (*Contrat nouvelle embauche*: New Job Contract).

the general private-sector system, thus implying cuts in these special regimes. The reform even secured the support of a certain number of trade unionists, academics and intellectuals traditionally considered as 'on the left'.[35] Yet there was massive opposition to the reform, and it transformed into a movement against neoliberal reforms in general. This allowed the movement not only to unite the popular classes within the left-wing bloc, but also to gather the support of private-sector workers. These latter supported a movement such as they had not themselves been capable of mounting two years earlier when their own pensions had been at stake.

For the right, the pursuit of neoliberal transformations thus implied a need to take account of the contradictory demands of the various components of its social base. It had to mediate between the hopes of economic liberalization, coming from the self-employed, and the fears expressed by private-sector workers. After all, for these latter, drastic changes in the French labour-market and social-protection models would bring increased insecurity in their status and finances.

Chirac's second term as president illustrated the difficulty of finding a compromise. Part of the right-wing bloc expressed its discontent towards the president's supposed 'immobilism' or lack of 'political courage' in the affair relating to the CPE (*Contrat première embauche*: First Job Contract).

His successor, Nicolas Sarkozy, was conscious of the fact that a return to Thatcher-style liberalization was very risky. He tried to find a new compromise between the divergent interests within the right-wing bloc – between the demand for flexibility and neoliberal reforms, on the one hand, and demands for protection, on the other. Sarkozy's quest for mediation thus led him to pursue two different approaches. The first was the promise of an eventual increase in purchasing power thanks to an increased supply of work: 'Work more to earn more' was one of Sarkozy's slogans during the 2007 election campaign. This took

---

35 Two petitions show that the fracture in the left-wing bloc also took place among the intellectuals themselves: one, for 'a fundamental reform of social security', defended (despite certain 'questionable aspects') 'a fundamental reform which work[ed] in the direction of social justice'. The other, an 'Intellectuals' appeal in support of the strikers', supported the strike movement, which represented 'a defence of the most universal conquests of the Republic'.

the form of lower taxes on overtime pay and a loosening of regulations on extra hours. Such a strategy had the advantage that it hollowed out part of the content of the reform to establish a thirty-five-hour week, but without abolishing it entirely. At the same time, it maintained or even extended the measures regarding flexibility in the organization of work,[36] which had represented part of the give-and-take between government and unions during the Jospin administration's implementation of this earlier thirty-five-hours reform.

The second approach was to assure voters that the path followed by the flexibilization of the labour market would be a flexicurity *à la française*, and not flexibility pure and simple, on the Anglo-Saxon model. To this end, in his speech to the Senate on 17 September 2007, Sarkozy declared that his strategy was guided by two principles:

> The first principle consists of putting work and employment at the heart of our social policies ... The second principle is the reconciliation of mobility and security, for employees as well as for businesses ... More security, for the employee, is the assurance that job loss will no longer be a drama and that episodes of unemployment, when they do happen, will be short and without negative consequence for the next phase of his career.

More concretely, the transformation of employment relations under Sarkozy was based on two types of reforms: a) the abolition of fixed-length and open-ended contracts in favour of a single flexible labour contract, with redundancy compensation that would increase over the course of time (flexibility); b) an 'occupational social security' that would guarantee generous compensation to the jobless, but also harden the obligation to accept job offers made by the 'public employment service' (this was the security part).

The compromise Sarkozy had dreamed up did not work – and for two reasons. The single-contract proposal did not satisfy the demands for flexibility coming from bosses, who sought to preserve atypical contracts and to increase flexibility across all labour contracts. But it

---

36   Measures regarding the counting (annualization) of working time.

also encountered the sharp hostility of most of the unions, which – not without reason – saw this as a generalized attack on the protection attached to the open-ended labour contract. Supported neither from the bosses' side nor by the unions, this timidly planned reform ended up at an impasse. Another factor would also put an end to the nebulous projects for a flexicurity *à la française*: the 2008 economic crisis. The weakening of economic activity, and then of the public finances, following the financial crisis – and then, the decision to opt for austerity – threw up obstacles to any possibility of implementing the 'security' part of the reform project.

We can thus see that, for at least three decades, the right has had no real strategy for mediating between the heterogenous expectations present within the social alliance it represents. In the absence of such a strategy, it swings back and forth between sporadic neoliberal offensives and retreats into positions that we could almost characterise as social-democratic, if this term had not lost all meaning in the recent political debate. Its problem is that a neoliberal rupture – especially if it was advanced by the right – would be difficult to carry through in any 'calm' manner.[37] Either it resolves to carry through such a rupture, knowing that the costs for this would be paid also by a fraction of its own base, or it gives up on such a project. Thus far it has largely taken this latter course: as we shall see, the main neoliberal reforms in France have been carried out by governments of the 'left'. But, in shying from such a rupture, the right has accelerated the leakage of its own voters towards the Front National, whose rise in the 1980s and 1990s is to be explained in terms of the disappointment of the 'neoliberal' fraction of the right-wing bloc – which is, at least partly, also the most *populaire* – namely artisans, traders and small businessmen.

THE SPLINTERING OF THE LEFT-WING BLOC

We will return at some length to the rupturing of the left-wing bloc. It is worth recalling here that, in the 1970s, this bloc was principally composed of public-sector managers and employees, blue-collar categories

---

37   In the 2007 campaign, Sarkozy's slogan spoke of a 'calm rupture'.

in general, and intellectual professions.[38] Its chances of success were –
as in the case of the right-wing bloc – tied to its capacity to combine
the support of these groups with that of a majority of private-sector
employees. Political mediation within the left-wing alliance centred
on social protection and rising purchasing power for lower-skilled
wage earners.

But, from the 1980s onwards, a project for 'modernizing' French
society emerged within the Parti Socialiste – a project with much
older roots. This project, which we will revisit in Chapter 2, met with
the support of only a minority of the left-wing bloc – namely, its
better-educated and more well-off section. Commitment to European
integration served the legitimation and strengthening of such a strategy, which was based on a minority of society. For thirty-five years, the
Parti Socialiste has presented the 'modernization' of the economy in
terms of responding to European 'constraints' – and thus the rupture
in the left-wing bloc has taken place over the European question. In
election campaigns, the Parti Socialiste has always tried to obtain the
support of the left-wing bloc. Yet, once in government, it has system-
atically abandoned part of its own electoral programme, in the name
of Europe.

European integration is the red thread that allows us to understand
the Parti Socialiste's record of reneging on its electoral promises. This
record stretches from the 'turn' of 1983 to its acceptance of European
treaties that François Hollande had promised – during the presidential campaign, that is – to renegotiate.[39] This explains why the rupture
between the popular classes and the 'governmental' left has taken place
on the ground of the European question. The most striking episode in

---

38   For a more detailed characterization of the two blocs, see Bruno Amable, Elvire
Guillaud and Stefano Palombarini, *L'Économie politique du néolibéralisme. Le cas de la France
et de l'Italie* (Paris: Éditions Rue d'Ulm, 2012); Bruno Amable, *Structural Crisis and Institutional Change in Modern Capitalism: French Capitalism in Transition* (Oxford: Oxford
University Press, 2017).

39   'I will renegotiate the European Treaty resulting from the 9 December 2011 agreement, privileging growth and jobs and the reorientation of the European Central Bank's
role in this direction. I will propose the creation of Eurobonds. I will defend the full and
entire association of the European and national parliaments with these decisions.' François
Hollande, 'Mes 60 engagements pour la France' – a programme for the presidential election – 2012, p. 12.

this divorce was, without doubt, the 2005 referendum on the European Constitutional Treaty, in which 76 per cent of blue-collar workers' votes were for 'No'.[40] But the rupture in which the Parti Socialiste abandoned the political representation of the popular-class part of the left-wing bloc dates back to the 1980s. Indeed, we can see its salient traits already in the choices of the second and third Mauroy governments.

After the failure of the expansionist policy that followed Mitterrand's victory in 1981, the alternative posed was between a) pursuing an expansionist course in order to keep unemployment down, accepting the risk of increased inflation and exiting the European Monetary System (EMS); or b) remaining within the EMS, adopting a deflationary policy to preserve the parity of the franc, and accepting unemployment. Mitterrand went for the second option. This was not simply an economic choice but also a political one: the 'austerity turn' contradicted the expectations of the popular classes within the left-wing bloc. This turn thus implied accepting the risk that the popular classes would part ways with the dominant bloc – and, indeed, contemplating the possibility of new allies. This would doubtless mean a search for an alliance with the fraction of the middle classes that favoured some aspects of the left's programme but had reservations over nationalizations, strong state intervention in the economy and political alliances with the Parti Communiste. The economic-policy turn carried through in 1983–84 – a turn we will analyse in subsequent chapters – was thus also a political turning point, and the beginning of a quest for alliances with the social groups and political forces in the middle of the left–right split. The consequence has been that certain social groups traditionally attached to the left – indeed, those who have most suffered the effects of economic crisis – have gradually turned away from it, withdrawing their support little by little.

Like the right-wing parties, the Parti Socialiste was conscious of the risks of a rupture with its social base, and tried to find a middle route. This attempt can be summarized as a bid to mount an energetic neoliberalization in the domains which (rightly or wrongly) were not considered priorities for the consolidation of the left-wing bloc (the

40   Eurobaromètre, *La Constitution européenne: sondage post-référendum en France*, June 2005.

financial system, the market for goods and services), while preserving as much as possible the domains most essential to the existence of this bloc: employment regulation and social protection.

Certain extensions of employment protection, a preservation of public-sector employment levels, and the move to reduce the legal working week to thirty-five hours thus more or less implicitly came 'in exchange for' the profound transformations that affected the financial system and corporate governance in the 1980s and 1990s.

Indeed, the thirty-five-hour reform had ambiguities of its own. The reduction in the legal working week allowed for growing flexibilization in the organization of work patterns. The combined effect of these transformations found its ideological expression in the promotion of 'social liberalism' – and this meant nothing other than an unnatural alliance between neoliberal flexibility and the welfare state.[41] At the level of economic structures, the model of capitalism thus (poorly) defined was characterized above all by its untenable contradictions and the absence of positive complementarities between its various institutional forms – that is to say, the absence of the very complementarities that ground the coherence and stabilities of different economic models.[42]

At the political level, these contradictions became manifest in the simplest of ways. 'Modernization' – meaning the part-neoliberalization of the French social and economic model under PS guidance – weakened the left's social base. Not only did it drive the popular classes' desertion of the left; it simultaneously fuelled the emergence of a vote for non-traditional parties on both left and right, and, as we have seen, drove an increase in abstention.

'REFORMIST' STRATEGIES AND POLITICAL CRISIS

We have spoken of the popular classes' disaffection with the traditional expressions of political representation, both left and right. This disaffection originates not so much from a change of cultural values

---

41 Or, more accurately, a 'counter-structural' alliance.
42 See Bruno Amable, 'Institutional Complementarities in the Dynamic Comparative Analysis of Capitalism', *Journal of Institutional Economics* 12: 1 (2015).

as from the consequences of the economic reforms which have been enacted across almost four decades. Taken as a whole, the popular classes are the most likely to be negatively affected by the economic and social repercussions of the transformations induced in France's social and economic model. The flexibilization of the labour market makes the occupational situation of the lower-skilled more precarious; the fall-off in social services – or, more generally, the various reforms to social protection – have negatively affected the living standards and quality of life of the least well-off households; the opening up of goods and services to market competition threatens the situation of the self-employed and the least competitive small producers; and so on. We can note, moreover, that the popular classes' attitude towards the neoliberal transformation project is sometimes more ambiguous than either agreement or unanimous rejection. Some groups may back parts of the project and reject others: artisans complain of the opening up of market competition in goods and services even as they demand the deregulation of the labour market. Lower-skilled groups of workers will fear this same deregulation process, while looking positively on some measures dismantling the welfare state – which, they hope, will only negatively affect other people.

These factors make it all the more difficult to seek mediation within either the left- or the right-wing bloc. As we have seen, the right-wing strategy has mainly played out within the dimension of labour flexibility, which is supposedly compensated by an extra supplement of security. As for the Parti Socialiste, only belatedly, after 2012, did it turn towards the option of 'flexicurity'. Its attempts at mediation were instead organized rather more around the question of European integration. Its key idea was to suggest that a reorientation of the European project could render the aspirations of the left's social base compatible with the 'modernization' of the French model – a 'modernization' process itself supposed to result from the constraints resulting from European integration.

As we shall go on to explain, we should instead privilege another interpretation of the PS's unfailing commitment to 'Europe'. Far from placing its hopes in 'another Europe', the PS's pursuit of European integration is, it hopes, a solution to the problem of the fragmentation of its own social base. This hope is rooted in the understanding that the party might consolidate a renewed social base precisely on the basis of the European project. Its commitment to European integration is functional not only to the 'modernisation' of the French model, thanks to the implementation of purportedly 'indispensable reforms', but also to a recomposition of the political landscape. This would mean blowing up the left–right divide, allowing it to bring together a new social bloc.

It should also be understood that the question of 'values' brought up by Terra Nova can itself be read as functional to this project. Emphasizing that the values of the 'new left' are the values of cosmopolitanism and cultural freedom – with solidarity and equality no longer counted among them – is a way of attracting the most well-off and well-educated part of the right-wing bloc towards the 'new left'. It aims to attract the part of the right-wing bloc which itself favours European integration and 'structural reforms', at the same time as it excludes the popular classes.

CHAPTER 2

The Parti Socialiste's Identity, at the Heart of the Crisis

For some, it was a betrayal – for others, just a recognition of the reality of the laws of economics. But for everyone it was a 'turning point'. The year 1983 marked the 'conversion' to neoliberalism of a Parti Socialiste that had arrived in power in 1981 with the ambition of profoundly transforming the structures of the French economy through the application of a Keynesian-inspired (and even partly Marxist) economic programme. Yet the very different economic-policy orientation that arrived two years after Mitterrand's election victory – an orientation that had in fact already won out in 1982 – represented a change that was far from sudden. The choices now being made were those already preferred by a major current within the Parti Socialiste – a current with a long history. Faced with an economic recovery programme that had been enacted against the spirit of the times – at the very moment when other developed countries were implementing austerity policies – and the imbalances which this logically enough produced (especially in the foreign trade balance), this current was able to grasp the opportunity to discredit any 'left-wing' economic policy. The turn to austerity was not, therefore, in any sense a conversion: rather, it corresponded to a shift in the internal equilibrium within the Parti Socialiste and the victory of a political line that had long been present within the party. Indeed, if we go back a bit further in time, we can retrace its origins.

THE ROOTS OF THE 'TURN': NEOLIBERALISM AND MODERNISM

Economic liberalism as an ideology entered into crisis at the end of the nineteenth century. In that period, it appeared incapable of accounting for the evolutions taking place in capitalism, and it was increasingly perceived as the ideology of the ruling classes, of the maintenance of the status quo and the dogged defence of the privileges of the wealthy. The 1929 crisis would further aggravate its discrediting. The idea, for half a century present even within liberal circles, that it was necessary to surpass liberalism rapidly spread among intellectuals and ruling elites. The 1920s and 1930s were thus an era characterized by the search for an ideological renewal, marked by the emergence of new political projects.[1]

We usually distinguish between two types of attempt to overcome the impasses of classical liberalism and 'laissez-faire': that of the 'new liberalism', associated with the names of Hobhouse or Keynes, and then another slightly later one, neoliberalism.[2] The latter is characterized by its denial of the natural character of the market; indeed, the (neo)liberals instead thought of the market as a social construct. Competition remains the fundamental pillar of a market economy, not only because it guarantees economic efficiency, but also on account of its supposed moral properties.[3] Competition allows – in theory, of course – a fight against privileges and unearned incomes based on position: it is only in a competitive regime that the most deserving are recompensed at the merited level.

Neoliberalism preserved traditional liberalism's idea that the market economy is the preferred way of organizing production and exchange. But it also took into account the active role that the state must play in the construction and preservation of a competitive order. Such an order would not emerge if the authorities limited themselves to laissez-faire among private actors. Many neoliberal authors use the metaphor of the highway code:

> To be a neoliberal is not to allow vehicles to circulate in all directions as they please, in a 'Manchesterian' sense, which would lead to incessant blockages and accidents; it is not to fix the departure time

---

1   François Denord, *Néolibéralisme version française. Histoire d'une idéologie politique* (Paris: Demopolis, 2007).

2   Pierre Dardot and Christian Laval, *The New Way of the World: On Neoliberal Society* (London: Verso, 2014).

3   Bruno Amable, 'Morals and Politics in the Ideology of Neo-Liberalism', *Socio-Economic Review* 9: 1 (2011), pp. 3–30.

and route of each vehicle, in the 'plannerist' sense; it is to impose a highway code, admitting that it is not necessarily the same in the time of powered transport as it was in the time of stagecoaches[4]

This last point corresponds to another major theme of neoliberalism, namely the need to adapt to a world in perpetual evolution, particularly in technological terms. This theme strongly colours Walter Lippmann's book *The Good Society*, a work whose French translation led to a conference which marked the real birth of neoliberalism in France.[5] Writing in 1937, Lippmann thought that, throughout their lives, individuals would have to move to a different occupation several times, and must therefore be prepared to change careers through an appropriate education policy. This argument would frequently re-emerge in economic policy debates even eighty years later. But now it would be presented as a radical novelty, breaking with the usual expectations of the 'Trente Glorieuses' [the "thirty glorious years" of post-war growth and interventionist economic policy].

Another current, 'modernism', developed in parallel to neoliberalism. Again, it took root in the critique of a traditional liberalism that was to be renewed rather than fought. Modernism originated from economic and administrative elites' perception that France was both economically and technologically running behind its neighbouring and competitor countries – both rivals and potential allies. After all, in 1870 French GDP per capita stood at only 50 per cent of the UK figure and 83 per cent of Germany's.[6] In 1913, it had caught up somewhat: by now, French GDP per capita reached 73 per cent of the US figure (which had itself overtaken the UK in this regard in the late nineteenth century) and 93 per cent of the German level. But the inter-war period did not see this tendency continue – quite the opposite. In 1938, French GDP per capita amounted to 69 per cent of the US figure and 82 per cent of Germany's.

---

4   See François Denord, 'La "modernisation" avant la lettre: le patronat français et la rationalisation (1925–1940)', *Sociétés contemporaines* 6: 4 (2007).

5   Walter Lippmann, *The Good Society* (London: George Allen & Unwin, 1937).

6   Calculation based on Stephen Broadberry's EuroGDP2 data, at nuffeld.ox.ac.uk, accessed June 2016.

We can better understand why this theme of modernization was attractive if we set it in the context of a certain French obsession revolving around the country's decline and belated adaptation. These factors, in turn, should be placed in relation to public interventions understood alternatively (or even simultaneously) as the cause of the problem and as a possible solution to it. This is a very old obsession, but it remains present even in contemporary political debate.

If the political centrality of the theme of decline emerged far earlier, American historian Richard Kuisel maintains that the origins of modernism go back to the inter-war period: the first attempts to impose it as the guideline directing economic policy date to the 1930s.[7]

The difficulties that France's productive base faced in sustaining the war effort during World War I sparked reflection that would have a major impact on modernism's ideological contours. During the conflict, state intervention appeared necessary in order to organize national production and supply chains abroad, since private firms were considered incapable of meeting the requirements of a war economy. This situation made clear the pertinence of critiques pointing to the inefficiency of laissez-faire, which had already been expressed during the first 'crisis of liberalism'. For the modernists who criticized 'individualist capitalism', laissez-faire led to an anarchic situation that put brakes on progress – all the more so because this liberalism, ideologically hostile to state intervention, gladly accommodated to protections that sheltered producers from international competition. Moreover, the experience of World War I – in which the trade unions had become associated with the war effort – showed how a social truce could serve productivity growth. Here, too, laissez-faire, with its active neglect of the social question, fell short of what was needed.

Engineers (especially those from the École Polytechnique) and industrialists – who together formed the core of the various movements attached to modernism before World War II – eagerly imagined a situation in which rationalist principles of corporate management could be transposed into the administration of the economy as a whole.

---

7   Richard Kuisel, *Capitalism and the State in Modern France: Renovation and Economic Management in the Twentieth Century* (Cambridge: Cambridge University Press, 1983).

Neocapitalism, for example, brought together industrialists who supported the spread of the scientific organization of work and of modern management methods, as opposed to the archaism of the traditional French *patronat*.[8] Here, too, we can identify a wish to take the methods for the rational management of private firms and apply them also in the public sector. The various movements (Ernest Mercier's Redressement français, Auguste Detœuf's journal *Nouveaux Cahiers*, Jean Coutrot's Groupe X-Crise, and so on) all had one important element in common. For each of them, the modernization of the economy would only be possible given the presence of an active state – the only actor capable of a long-term vision – whose role would, however, also have to be defined and conceived in partnership with private initiative. On the one hand, it was necessary to strengthen the powers of technocratic administration, indispensable for organizing and providing orientation to private initiatives. On the other hand, there was no question of allowing voter expectations and the demands for protection coming from *particular* interests to condition the development strategy too directly: parliament's powers thus had to be reduced.

They thus shared the perspective of a competent technocratic elite, to be put in charge of upholding the general interest. This was itself understood in terms of the modernization of techniques, the spread of rational management methods and, more generally, as a renewal of economic structures. The rationalization of the productive machine was meant to allow an increase in living standards, and thus a response to the social question liberalism had mistakenly neglected. Productivity growth would especially benefit the poorest classes, which would thus help turn the toiling masses away from any revolutionary temptations. The modernist project was thus, at once, a transition to an enlightened capitalism, overcoming the inadequacies of laissez-faire, and, at the same time, a rampart against the socialist or even communist tendencies of a working class whose 'understandable' needs would be satisfied by a gradual and 'reasonable' increase in its living standards.

The modernists' technocratic ideal did not stop them from singing the praises of social dialogue. Yet this dialogue was conceived not as

---

8   See Denord, 'La "modernisation" avant la lettre'.

the search for compromise between divergent interests, but rather as a phase one had to pass through in order to overcome 'ideological' stances and allow the unanimous embrace of the strategy that corresponded to the general interest. The social dialogue advocated by the modernists was supposed to aid the toiling masses' conversion to the religion of efficiency and progress linked to new management methods and production techniques, whose fruits, modernism promised, would be shared far and wide.

Modernism and neoliberalism thus shared major elements in common. They were each grounded in the wish to renew liberalism through a critique of traditional laissez-faire, overcoming any opposition between state and market. The two currents differed in terms of what they saw as the objectives of public intervention: whereas, for the modernists, the goal was the long-term improvement of economic structures, for the neoliberals, it was a matter of preserving competitive market organization. The modernists and neoliberals shared a common distrust of the mechanisms of democratic politics, since these drew too much attention either to short-term expectations (as the modernists saw it) or to specific interest groups' demands for limits on competition (as the neoliberals saw it). Another dominant element in both movements was their elitism. The modernists thought that technical competence alone provided the legitimacy to take decisions; the neoliberals saw competition as the mechanism that would allow the 'intrinsic superiorities' of individual capabilities to replace the 'extrinsic inequalities' owing to privileges.[9]

Modernists and neoliberals, moreover, opposed those movements that proposed a way out of capitalism – even if this was only a distant and notional horizon. They thus shared not only anticommunist sentiment, but also an opposition to socialism and any political current that counted Marxism among its theoretical reference points.

More simply, we often find the same individuals both involved in modernist circles and at the origins of neoliberalism. For example, the modernists August Detœuf and Louis Marlio figured among the participants in the conference on Walter Lippmann's book, which served

---

9   Lippmann, *Good Society*.

as the launch-pad for neoliberalism in France; and another modernist, Jacques Branger of Groupe X-Crise, considered that the alternative to either the directed economy or Manchesterian laissez-faire could be called 'neoliberalism'.

Modernism had a relatively limited impact on the determination of economic policies before World War II. We can detect a certain modernist inspiration during the war, both in the Vichy government and in the provisional government in London.[10] But the French economy's great modernist era was the post–World War II period: its importance in setting the orientations of post-war French economic policy is well-known.

Modernism also had an impact on the structuring of the political supply, on both the right and the left. If modernism's own greatest political exponent was Pierre Mendès-France, the 'age of modernists' above all came with the Fifth Republic.[11] The *dirigisme* of the Gaullist period was, indeed, what Kuisel calls a 'neoliberal order'.[12] The term *dirigisme* is itself ambiguous; it can correspond to the vision of an economy under the *orders* of some directing force, or to one to which some direction is *indicated*. This latter best corresponds to the way in which economic policy was really conducted in France during the era of indicative planning. As Jean Fourastié put it, coining a phrase rather reminiscent of the neoliberal 'highway code' metaphor, this planning operated as a road-map indicating possible routes, without making the choice of any particular one compulsory.[13]

In post-war modernist ideology, we find elements that were already present in the pre-war period, notably the ideal of an enlightened technocracy whose legitimacy in terms of the structuring economic choices was supposedly superior to that of political actors themselves.[14] The vision of Europe as a modernizing force, and of international

---

10   Denord, 'La "modernisation" avant la lettre'.

11   André Gauron, *Histoire économique et sociale de la Cinquième République, vol. I: Le Temps des modernistes* (Paris, La Découverte/Maspero, 1983).

12   Kuisel, *Capitalism and the State in Modern France*.

13   Julie Bouchard, *Comment le retard vient aux Français. Analyse d'un discours sur la recherche, l'innovation et la compétitivité. 1940–1970* (Lille, Presses universitaires du septentrion, 2008).

14   Pierre Bourdieu and Luc Boltanski, 'La production de l'idéologie dominante', *Actes de la recherche en sciences sociales*, 1976 (2).

competition as a factor that would energize the productive base, was also partly the inheritance of positions like those of *Nouveaux Cahiers* and Redressement Français. Already in the inter-war period, they had supported a project of European unity based on economic terms, in order to rationalize production at a continental scale and, as an accessory to this, to build a rampart against the USSR.

There was total continuity between the pre- and post-war modernists when it came to rejecting 'extremes'. For instance, Ernest Mercier's Redressement Français called robustly for a stable republican government that would include all political forces except the PCF, the Socialist SFIO and the far right; we may also note that, as he sought investiture to the prime minister's office in 1954, Mendès France refused to count on Communist votes. The charges levelled against traditional liberalism – including its 'Malthusianism'; distrust for social movements, combined with a privileging of 'social dialogue'; and the notion of capitalist development guided by an enlightened technocracy – all helped feed the modernists' commitment to a re-foundation of the left and the unions on a new, anti-Marxist and anti-communist basis.

Modernist ideology that served as a bridge between the 'non-communist' left and the right – in particular for Jacques Delors, a member of prime minister Chalban-Delmas's cabinet in 1969, economy and finance minister for François Mitterrand between 1981 and 1984. He would also be president of the European Commission at the moment of the completion of the Common Market, the liberalization of finance, and the beginning of monetary unification, a process that would ultimately lead to the single currency: the euro. His political project combined the classic themes of modernism: namely, the rejection of 'extremes' – which, for the 'governmental left', ultimately meant a refusal to compromise with parties to the left of a PS, itself drifting ever further to the right; an emphasis on 'competence' in economic matters, translating into adherence to neoliberal economic dogmas; the desire to privilege 'social dialogue' rather than binding legislation – and so on. From Mendès France to Macron via Delors, the modernism of the 'governmental left' continued to degenerate, abandoning whatever social concerns it might originally have had, and only retaining those elements it shared with neoliberalism.

The 'Second Left' was the natural heir of the modernist experience: decentralizing, pro-self-management and elitist, it allied with a left of dirigiste and Marxist traditions in the Parti Socialiste. Within that party, it mounted a struggle that would result in its own crushing victory.

THE IDEOLOGICAL VICTORY OF THE SECOND LEFT

Heir to the modernist experience, the Second Left has always been a force present within the Parti Socialiste, ever since that party's creation in 1971. The Second Left privileged contracts and negotiation over legislative interventions; hostile to nationalizations, it rejected Marxist reference points and opposed direct state involvement in the economy; nursing a highly critical vision of national sovereignty, it stood for a federal Europe; its natural allies were centrists rather than the Parti Communiste. But the institutions of the Fifth Republic – and the structuring of the 'supply' side of the political market that resulted – made such an alliance impossible.

The Second Left would long remain a minority within PS ranks, though by no means was it a marginal force. At the Metz Congress in 1979, its leading figure openly advocated 'economic realism', the centrality of businesses and the need to support them: 'Liberal thought is in crisis … but so, too, is socialist thought, because it dares not embrace the inverse need: to recognise that the act of production needs motivations other than constraint. A rigid centralised planning will not be enough for us.' His motion only picked up 20.4 per cent support at the Congress, but the motion put forward by Pierre Mauroy, who stood very close to the Second Left on economic issues, won 13.6 per cent.[15] Thus, in 1979, at least one-third of PS members backed an economic policy approach that was far from hostile to the 'market economy' and so-called 'economic realism'.

The relation of forces evolved further after the PS came to power at the beginning of the 1980s. The 'turn' in the Socialists' policies in 1983 corresponded to the Second Left's ideological victory within the party,

---

15   See Mathieu Fulla, *Les Socialistes français et l'économie (1944–1981). Une histoire économique du politique* (Paris: Presses de Sciences Po, 2016).

at least in terms of the primary importance of 'economic realism'. Thus, the general policy speech that Prime Minister Laurent Fabius gave to the National Assembly on 24 July 1984 was strongly inspired by the Second Left's preferred themes – indeed, it was almost an ode to modernism. 'To modernise and to bring together: these are the priorities of the government I lead', Fabius began, continuing:

> The battle for employment must be fiercely fought, but it can only be won on the basis of a modern economy. My approach is as follows: any real improvement in employment passes by way of a certain growth; all durable growth supposes a solid productive base able to export and to defend its positions on the domestic market; any solid productive base needs to be modern in order to withstand competition. It was because the French economy was not yet sufficiently modernised in 1974 that my predecessor Mr Chirac failed in his attempt to kick-start growth in 1975. Seven years later, it was because our economy was not sufficiently modernised that we had to stop the [expansive plan] and devalue. The fight against unemployment will doubtless be long and difficult because modernization – we should have the honesty to say it – may cost jobs before it creates more ... to refuse to modernise would cost more jobs than anything else, because we would be left uncompetitive.[16]

Hence, once again, the choice was between 'modernization or decline'.[17] Fabius indicated that 'three fundamental actions will decide the future of our economy ... [r]esearch, training, investment. That goes for industry, for agriculture, for fishing, for artisan trades and for commerce. It goes for metropolitan France as for its overseas territories. These [three] are the triangle at the basis of modernisation'. The modernist position with regard to social dialogue was similarly embraced, indeed wholesale: 'Economic inefficiency is inseparable from social dialogue ... my wish is that the social partners should conduct, at the

---

16   'Discours de Laurent Fabius à l'Assemblée nationale', 24 July 1984, at archives. gouvernement.fr.

17   'Modernisation or Decline' was the title of the first plan presented by Jean Monnet, in 1946.

national but also company level, a common reflection on the conditions in which social progress can contribute to the competitiveness of our companies and to growth.'

The Second Left's victory – and the break from the Marxist reference point that had been present within the PS in previous years – fully shone through in Fabius's comments on the role of the state and the central importance he attributed to business: 'There will be no successful economic modernization without a concomitant modernization of social relations; but that is not something that can be decreed. So, what role for the state? What place for business? What content for contractual policy?', Fabius asked in his address to the Assembly. His answers could not have been clearer:

> The state's role is not to impose what the country does not want, or to prevent what it aspires to, but to make possible what is necessary … The responsibility for modernization essentially lies with businesses. They must, therefore, enjoy the support of the whole country. I have always thought that it was the left that was best placed to reconcile business and nation … So, let us clearly put our trust in businesses' ability … Let us put our trust in the staff, up and down hierarchy, who are the very reality of the business. It is they, in their diversity, who will determine the success or failure of the development of our economy. Here, as elsewhere, success will deserve recognition and recompense.

A few months later, the need for the Socialists to 'modernize' – which involved getting rid of certain prehistoric taboos – was reasserted in a column in *Le Monde* signed by four young PS members, including a certain François Hollande. 'The dogmatic conception of the working class, the idea that the workplace could also be a space of freedom, the notion that individuals belong to solid social groups, the affirmation of a timeless political programme – all this must be abandoned', wrote Hollande and his co-authors. 'The Parti Socialiste is doubtless the country's foremost workers' party, but should it not aspire also to be the party of the whole society? It should thus address itself to individuals as well as groups, appealing far more to realities than to myths, and adopt a modest approach – which does not mean

a meagre one, but rather an approach adapted to the times to come'.
They continued:

> Far from being absent, the state retains a fundamental role. It must
> perfect the effectiveness of its interventions so that 'things work' and
> the growing anxieties of the French are thus reduced ... In this period
> of uncertainty, where the desire for understanding is manifest, it must
> also anticipate, foresee, herald future developments, in short, be a
> 'state that shines a light on the way ahead'.[18]

This column should be credited as running far ahead of the proposal
for a 'left of values' formulated by Terra Nova almost thirty years later.[19]
'The left', wrote Hollande in 1984,

> is not an economic project but a system of values. It is not a way of
> producing but a way of being. It is modern when it is itself – which
> is to say, first of all democratic ... Democracy, the necessary mar-
> riage between freedom – notably the freedom to be different – and
> the equality of rights and opportunities, is the only suitable way of
> embracing technological change.

The left's very survival would 'depend on its capacity firstly to "restructure" itself, in order to make society as a whole accept modernization'.
Before he arrived in power, Mitterrand had declared that the
choice was between capitalism and socialism; at the Épinay Congress
he had expressed his view that one could be a member of the PS only if
one accepted the 'rupture' with capitalist society.[20] But, in the space of a

---

18   The column published in *Le Monde* on 16 December 1984 was titled 'Pour être
modernes, soyons démocrates'. It was signed by François Hollande, Jean-Yves Le Drian,
Jean-Michel Gaillard and Jean-Pierre Mignard.

19   See the analysis of the Terra Nova report in Chapter 1.

20   'We could not arbitrarily separate General de Gaulle from the type of society
he embodies. To fight the one compelled us to fight the other. They went hand-in-hand.
The essential thing did not consist of destroying the new organization of politics, in many
domains superior to the old one because it took more account of the requirements of stability and continuity, necessary for long-term plans in a socialist society as in a capitalist
society. It was to get directly to the point, to relentlessly attack the centres of economic
decision-making, to destroy the strongroom where the monopolies had sheltered their levers

few years, the PS passed from this to Fabius's claim that the left had to reconcile business and nation, and to the young Hollande fighting for the ditching of any idea that the workplace could also become a space of freedom and that the left was identified with an economic project.

The PS would never really question the modernist line again. Moreover, at the end of Mitterrand's second term in 1995, the party planned a presidential run by a major figure in the party's 'reformist' wing, Jacques Delors. We will note in passing his decisive role in anchoring modernist thinking within the party. A member of the Club Jean-Moulin in the 1960s, in 1969 he joined modernist Prime Minister Jacques Chaban-Delmas's cabinet under Georges Pompidou's presidency, and then became economy and finance minister in the first left-wing governments after 1981, and president of the European Commission up until 1995.[21] A determined partisan of so-called 'economic realism', in November 1981 he called for a 'pause' in the left-wing reforms. We will return to this in the next chapter. In between two posts (as minister and Commission president), in 1985, he wrote a book entitled *En sortir ou pas*, together with the journalist Philippe Alexandre. This was a vehement critique of the Union de la Gauche's economic policy, a defence of austerity, and an appeal to seek a political alliance that could unite 'wise men of all sides' in supporting the economic policy it so strongly appealed for: the rehabilitation 'of the market, business, profit, and bosses', since 'a society progresses also thanks to its inequalities'.[22]

---

of command. To proceed any other way would have meant embarking upon the same errors [that followed] Liberation and losing the wood for the trees. There was not a choice between the Fourth and Fifth Republic but between capitalism and socialism. That is what I concluded after a long debate. You asked me, what is the left? Now, it is socialism' François Mitterrand, *Ma part de vérité. De la rupture à l'unité* (Paris: Fayard, 1969).

21   The Club Jean-Moulin brought together top civil servants from the 'non-communist left' and aimed to contribute to a debate on modern democracy and orient public policy choices through the promotion of 'technical competence'. It adopted the well-known stance of rejecting both liberal capitalism and centralized planning in favour of democratic planning and a mixed economy. The Club's charter featured the usual elements of modernist ideology: the end of 'ideologies', involving workers in company administration, the promotion of competence, distrust towards parliament, and so on. See Claire Le Strat and Willy Pelletier, *La Canonisation libérale de Tocqueville* (Paris: Syllepse, 2005)

22   Philippe Alexandre and Jacques Delors, *En sortir ou pas* (Paris: Grasset, 1983), pp. 122, 64, respectively.

Selections from Philippe Alexandre and Jacques Delors, *En sortir ou pas*, Paris, Bernard Grasset, 1985

'All countries have committed, by will or by compulsion, to an economic battle both joyous and wild. But France hesitates and quivers: it is not prepared to admit that the world dictates its law by way of the economy' (p. 19).

'Only under the Raymond Barre government did the French begin to grasp the reality, to understand that their fate was playing out outside their own borders, firstly in Europe and then in the world. Sadly there still exists even in enlightened minds this archaic idea that France can escape this by itself ... Arriving in power in 1981, the left was in large measure a victim of this illusion [that it could] take another path and refuse to follow our European neighbours' (p. 21).

'The French ... declare themselves convinced that there exists no miraculous recipe for dealing with this crisis ... This scepticism, full of common sense, translates into the desire to see wise men of all sides come together and join all layers and categories of society in one effort' (pp. 27–8).

'Disfigured by the void in the centre, political representation in France is still disfigured by the exorbitant influence that the extremists exert on both left and right: communism, and populism' (p. 33).

'The Communists ... have had an influence on the Socialists which will leave lasting traces: they have made them, or at least many of them, thus predisposed by a religious attachment to Marxism, share their vision of French society, their refusal to consider the crisis in its planetary dimension, their aversion towards austerity [*rigueur*] (pp. 33–4).

'The crisis has produced a miracle: for administering the economy imposes a certain restraint on the prophets of an untamed liberalism and of exemplary socialism. Market constraints ... drove the polemicists to yield to the experts. A connection has been re-established with businesses, now considered by all as the leaders of the forced march towards the future. No one ... is still treated as an "aberrant product of the bourgeoisie" when he sings the praises of profit. But the economic compromise is yet to find its translation in the social and political domains' (p. 34).

'[T]he rupture with capitalism is a myth propped up by the French Socialists since their first emergence' (p. 47).

'[I]t is the left in power, which, at the cost of a dazzling and cruel revolution, will re-establish companies' profits and make the French understand that enterprise must prosper and enjoy beneficial margins for investing, for taking initiative, for creating employment ... It will be left up to the right ... To make good use of this apprenticeship in economic realities which the French have now completed (p. 48).

'The protection which our societies have dispensed to our citizens will have had, as its first result, their weakening' (p. 55).

'Heavy, rigid, out of proportion, the social protection system is constantly added to and further complicated: it lays the basis for abuses ... Unemployment compensation, in France as in all European countries, constitutes nothing less than a powerful incentive not to work' (p. 56).

'Our countries could one day regret having taken on the burden of such expensive social security. That day has come' (pp. 57–8).

'The striking truth: to turn exclusively to the state to fulfil the duties incumbent upon each of us, to substitute individual solidarity with national solidarity, is not a sign of progress' (p. 59).

'Most of the sick would doubtless prefer to be less examined and analysed but more surrounded and loved' (p. 59).

'We really should do away with this taboo of an absolute social protection, equal for all' (p. 61).

'[A] society progresses also thanks to its inequalities' (p. 64).

'[The French citizen] is torn from his illusions by realities just as sovereign and unchangeable as the stars in the night sky: market, business, the risk factor in success, international competition ... which one cannot escape' (p. 69).

'No one can free themselves of the tough law of competition' (p. 69).

'Now, capital is less taxed in France than labour is. Thanks to the left. Nonsense, cried some in the Parti Communiste and also the PS' (p. 80).

'History will tell who – the pre-1981 utopians or the realists of 1982 and 1983 – is responsible for this sudden crisis of confidence on the left' (p. 84).

'In the United States, Reagan had all the difficulties in the world embarking upon a "deregulation", in untying the straitjacket of regulations and administrative texts which paralysed the economy' (p. 90).

'The functioning of the finance market has been so helped along [since 1982] that the Communists accuse the Socialists of having enriched the wealthy ... Really, now! The left was obliged to put investment and savings back on track' (p. 118).

'[A]ll the French must convert, as a matter of urgency, to the spirit of the market' (p. 123).

'Since 1982 the left in France has devoted body and soul to striving to rehabilitate the market, business and employers, to giving rise to stocks as savings, to chasing away the anticapitalist myth' (p. 125).

'The historic compromise has, as its goal, the organization of a calm exchange of power ... It seeks to rally all political actors who uphold neither dogmatic codes [la langue de bois] or the spirit of parochialism: some will go into government and others will form a constructive opposition, but neither will be considered renegades when they happen to express adjacent or identical ideas' (p. 212).

In spite of very favourable poll ratings, Delors refused to stand in the presidential election. This was partly due to personal reasons. But there were also political reasons of which it is interesting to remind ourselves, sine they go some way to explaining the difficulties of Hollande's presidency.[23]

For Delors, the decisive question was whether, once elected, he would have 'the opportunity and the political means to accomplish indispensable reforms'. These reforms were, indeed, oriented towards the supposed 'modernization' of the French economy and the deepening of European integration. As he concluded: 'the absence of a majority to support such a policy, whatever the measures taken after the election, would not allow me to put my solutions into effect'.[24]

In 1994, Delors considered the structure of the political 'supply' incompatible with his strategy. The Parti Socialiste and its allies were supported by a social bloc somewhat different from the one which would have corresponded to his own objectives. Delors could have won the election by basing himself on the left-wing bloc; but, once elected, he would have had to give up on reforms he considered 'indispensable', for want of any political and social majority to support them. He thus expressed regret at the absence of a social and political alliance different to that which the PS had formed over previous decades. His action in government would have been the victim of the split between the PS's economic (and ideological) objectives and the expectations of the left's electoral base – a divide to which we will return in Chapter 3.

If we look beyond French borders, we can see that, over the 1990s, the themes that characterized the French left had in fact become dominant across a large part of European social democracy. Elsewhere in Europe, the anti-Marxist left which saw the enterprise not as the heart of social conflict but the motor of economic progress did not bear the name 'Second Left' – instead it was called the 'Third Way' or even 'New Centre'. Thus, for the best-known theorist of the Third Way, Anthony Giddens, it was necessary to abandon the vision many socialists had of

---

23   Emmanuel Van Brabant, Lorenz Eberle, 'Entre péripétie électorale et vision politique, le non de Delors', *Mots* 45: 1 (1995).

24   Jacques Delors interviewed by Anne Sinclair on *7 sur 7*, 11 December 1994.

a providential state focused on equality.[25] For him, 'the collapse of socialism's historic ambitions' should lead to the transformation of the welfare state into a 'positive welfare'. This would mean pushing the individual to construct an 'autotelic self' allowing him to transform 'potential threats into rewarding challenges'. The task was no longer to protect against social risks, but rather to turn them into a positively felt 'active challenge'; similarly, the aim should be not the 'direct transfer of wealth' towards the poorest, but rather to increase their 'employment opportunities'.[26]

For Giddens and the Third Way, the social changes that have marked the evolution of capitalism over the last thirty years have rendered obsolete the traditional left–right cleavage based on state intervention in the economy (though, as we will go on to show, it is in fact very much still relevant in differentiating French voters' policy preferences). As he put it,

We now live in an economy largely dominated by knowledge industries and service industries, which have formed new social groups, very different to those of yesteryear. Today, we live in a very different society to that of thirty years ago, composed of new classes like white collar workers, neither office employees nor manual labourers, who spend their day exercising their savoir-faire on their computers. These employees look more like the middle class: they do not have a

---

25   Anthony Giddens, *Beyond Left and Right: The Future of Radical Politics* (Cambridge: Polity, 1994). 'For most socialists … the welfare state seemed to point up a way ahead to a controllable and egalitarian future, whether or not this was seen as a halfway house to "full socialism" or to some version of communism. With the collapse of socialism's historical ambitions, we have to look at the welfare state in quite a different light' (p. 150).

26   'Schemes of positive welfare, oriented to manufactured rather than external risk, would be directed to fostering the autotelic self. The autotelic self is one with an inner confidence which comes from self-respect, and one where a sense of ontological security, originating in basic trust, allows for the positive appreciation of social difference. It refers to a person able to translate potential threats into rewarding challenges, someone who is able to turn entropy into a consistent flow of experience. The autotelic self does not seek to neutralize risk or to suppose that "someone else will take care of the problem"; risk is confronted as the active challenge which generates self-actualization' (Giddens, *Beyond Left and Right*, p. 192). The new left should thus adopt 'a wide notion of welfare, taking the concept away from economic provision for the deprived towards the fostering of the autotelic self … The effort bargain with the poor would not be the direct transfer of wealth but a transfer of employment opportunities coming from changed attitudes towards work on the part of the more affluent' (ibid., pp. 194–5).

'class consciousness', they change career over the course of their lives, specializing, falling and climbing up the social ladder. They do not recognise themselves in the Left–Right debates of yesteryear. They think according to other, more individual criteria, more interested in modernity, the improvement of their lifestyle, the democratisation of social questions, security, urban policy, immigration and the environment, for instance.[27]

This political outlook, which holds that a declining working class can no longer be the left's main social referent, spread very widely among European social democracy in the course of the 1990s. This is, as we have seen, the vision advanced by Terra Nova in 2011; but it was already that of the modernists of the 1930s, of Rocard's Second Left in the 1970s, of the Parti Socialiste from the early 1980s, and also of the young Hollande in 1984.

Nonetheless, until 2012, there did remain one piece of French exceptionalism. Contrary to what was going on in many European countries, where the social-democratic left governed in the teeth of radical-left opposition – and sometimes in alliance with centrist (or even right-wing) parties – the Parti Socialiste renewed its alliance with the Parti Communiste. The Hollande presidency put an end to this exception. For the first time under the Fifth Republic, from 2012 the PS was in government while part of the parliamentary left remained in opposition. In this change, we can see the PS's alignment with European social democracy, but also a move to make its choice of allies consistent with the political line that had dominated in its ranks for over three decades.

The PS's course fully corresponded to the dominant ideology among its leading cadres. Yet, as we shall see, this also posed major problems in light of the expectations of the 'left's' electorate. The European question helped fragment these expectations, making any political mediation between the electors of the former left-wing bloc very difficult to identify.

---

27   Interview with Anthony Giddens published on Frédéric Joignot's blog on 15 October 2007: 'Le grand sociologue critique une "gauche française conservatrice"', lemonde. fr/blog/fredericjoignot, accessed June 2016.

THE EUROPEAN PROJECT IN SERVICE OF THE SOCIAL-LIBERAL TURN

The contradictions between European integration and the unity of the left-wing bloc have a long history. When the Left arrived in power in 1981 it was clear that two objectives – participation in European political and economic integration, and the unity of the social bloc built on the popular classes and public-sector employees – were likely to prove politically irreconcilable. This was especially, but not only, true in phases of economic slowdown.

As we shall see in Chapter 3, François Mitterrand – the strategist behind the Union de la Gauche – was the first to be confronted with this problem, soon after he came to power. On the one hand, he had to stick to his campaign promises, especially in terms of boosting the purchasing power of the poorest fraction of the waged workforce. The question of whether he would respect his electoral programme had a very particular political value – it is worth remembering that the convergence between the Communist and Socialist parties over common policy measures had required almost ten years of tense negotiations, marked by the Communist leaders' lack of confidence in a PS they considered scarcely trustworthy. On the other hand, the European monetary project, in this era being translated into the EMS, was based on a rigorous budgetary discipline. As François Stasse – an economic advisor to President Mitterrand from 1981 to 1984 – recalls, 'we were held to a certain discipline in our public accounts, and our partners made us respect it, sometimes vigorously so. This sharp candour was logical enough, for the very principle of EMS held that when one member was in difficulty the others would come to its aid by lending it the money it needed to finance its deficits.'[28]

Mitterrand thus found himself forced to choose. He could remain anchored to Europe and profoundly change his economic programme, which would imply disappointing the expectations of a major segment of the social base on which he had built his successful campaign; or, he could privilege the unity of the left-wing bloc, and resign himself to the franc exiting the EMS.

---

28 '1983: affronter la crise', interview with François Stasse published in *La Lettre de l'Institut François-Mitterrand*, 11 March 2005.

It is interesting to note that, at least according to many accounts from the time, Mitterrand did not attribute any great importance to his advisers' economic arguments – neither those that advocated the austerity turn that was later negotiated, nor those exalting the benefits of 'another policy'. For Mitterrand, this was much less a matter of identifying the more economically 'effective' solution than of choosing between two political objectives: the unity of the left and the renewal of the alliance with the Communists, or else Franco-German solidarity, which he considered essential, particularly faced with the Soviet threat. At the same time, as we pointed out earlier, the economy minister was Jacques Delors, a fervent supporter of European integration and a figure culturally close to the Second Left. The latter – emphasizing compromise and negotiation rather than social conflict – had never seen the Parti Communiste as its privileged ally. Moreover, Delors was also the minister who, having pursued the economic revival and nationalizations policy in the ephemeral 'grace period' that followed the Socialists' 1981 election victory, then took charge of implementing the policy of budget cuts, fighting inflation, and strengthening the franc that had been determined during the 'turn' of 1983. After that, in January 1985, he became President of the European Commission, which he went on to lead for some ten years, a period in which European integration took a resolutely neoliberal turn.[29]

The *political* choice was to decide against any action that might put the European project into question. The Parti Communiste would pay a heavy electoral price for participating in governments whose actions did not correspond either to its voters' preferences or to its campaign promises. Credited with 16.1 per cent support in the 1981 parliamentary elections (a score its leaders had judged disappointing), the PCF fell to 11.2 per cent in the 1984 European contest, then to 9.8 per cent at the 1986 parliamentary elections and 7.7 per cent in the 1989 European elections.

The history of the negotiations between Socialists and Communists in the 1970s sheds some light on Mitterrand's choice. Throughout

---

29   See François Denord and Antoine Schwartz, *L'Europe sociale n'aura pas lieu* (Paris: Raisons d'agir, 2009); Robert Salais, *Le Viol d'Europe. Enquête sur la disparition d'une idée* (Paris: PUF, 2013).

that decade, the Socialist leader displayed his great flexibility on both economic themes (nationalizations, democratic planning, consideration of macroeconomic balances) and his ideological reference points, from Marxist to 'Keynesian–Mendésist' and 'Keynesian–regulationist.'[30] The priority was to have a political agreement with the PCF, which was necessary for the PS to conquer power and determined the construction of the party's own internal majorities. However, from the first contacts between the two parties, it was clear that the PS was not prepared to negotiate on the European question.[31]

As Mathieu Fulla reminds us, in 1969 'the Communists reasserted their opposition to supranationalism. For them, the expansion of the Common Market risked locking "little Europe into subjection to the Atlantic Pact [NATO]". The Socialists replied by affirming their unbreakable support for the pursuit of European integration, even while recognizing that the form the Common Market had taken did not suit them.'[32] The Socialist position did not suffer from ambiguities. On nationalizations as on other economic matters, room for an agreement with the PCF could always be found, even at the cost of rather spectacular doctrinal about-turns. But such accommodations could not be made when it came to Europe.[33]

The choice made in 1983 thus continued in the same vein as the Socialists' prior trajectory. Fully in keeping with his previous positions, after coming to power Mitterrand showed great flexibility on questions of economic policy, even to the point of being able to negotiate the austerity turn without hesitation; yet the pursuit of European integration would remain an enduring priority. Moreover, Mitterrand had in all

30   See Fulla, *Les Socialistes français et l'économie*.

31   See 'Le premier bilan des conversations entre le Parti Socialiste et le Parti Communiste français', 22 December 1970, supplement to *La Documentation socialiste*, 17 December 1970.

32   Fulla, *Les Socialistes français et l'économie*, p. 238.

33   Without claiming to give any definitive explanation for the unfailing commitment that the dominant part of the SFIO and then PS made to Europe, we can simply mention that this project was at the intersection of two concerns of the 'non-Communist' left: the constitution of a continental bloc to face the Soviet threat, and an opening to international competition – a factor in the 'modernization' of the productive apparatus. However, some modernizers, even important ones like Mendès-France, very soon expressed doubts over the concrete process leading to the EEC, even while remaining loyal to the idea of European unity.

probability anticipated the need for such a turn even at the point that he took power in 1981:

> The voluntarist rhetoric that François Mitterrand and Pierre Mauroy used when they arrived in office was not accompanied by a CERES[34] invasion of the ministerial cabinets associated with the elaboration of economic policy. On the contrary, the president very quickly had word spread in Paris and the other European capitals that Jacques Delors was to be appointed to the Finance Ministry, in order to dispel fears concerning France's possible withdrawal from the [European] institutions … In late 1981, the recognition that the global recovery heralded by OECD and INSEE experts had not arrived as expected convinced the Socialist leaders – except the *chevènementistes* – that 'austerity with a human face' was an inevitable measure that had to be taken in the very short term. This was necessary in order to avoid a repeat of the scenario that played out in 1936 and 1956, namely a Socialism in government which was unable to leave a lasting mark of its efforts, because it did not manage to get a handle on the public finances.[35]

The referendum on Maastricht was the second episode that helps shed light on the relations between the left's strategies and the European question. The projects for monetary unification and fiscal harmonization were at the heart of Mitterrand's second term. For the Socialist president, there was no longer any need for the hesitations of a few years beforehand; the Maastricht Treaty was conceived and negotiated on Mitterrand's and Delors's own initiative. In 1988, Mitterrand secured an agreement in principle with the German chancellor, Helmut Kohl, on the creation of a single currency. The following year, he formed a working group led by Élisabeth Guigou, which brought together representatives of the finance and foreign ministries of the twelve states that were members of the European Community at that time. Its conclusions would provide the basis for the discussions of

---

34   Centre d'Études, de Recherches et d'Éducation Socialiste – the left current in the PS, led by Jean-Pierre Chevènement.

35   Fulla, *Les Socialistes français et l'économie*, p. 402.

the inter-governmental conference that led, in 1991, to the Maastricht Treaty.

After his experiences in government in the 1980s, Mitterrand could hardly have been unaware of the consequences that the new European rules would have for the unity of the left-wing bloc. Indeed, these rules were much more restrictive than those that had driven him to abandon his campaign promises in order to ensure the viability of the EMS in 1983. Even in its programmatic announcements, the Socialist position at the end of the 1980s was explicit: the priority objective was European unity, to which the possibility of uniting the left-wing bloc had to be sacrificed. The dropping of any Keynesian policies to kick-start the economy was expressed in 1993 through the definitive formula: 'We have tried everything to cut unemployment.'

But the Socialist administration's strategy was, in truth, rather more sophisticated. This was not a forced choice between a domestic policy objective (the identification of a compromise that would be satisfactory for the left's whole social base) and a foreign policy one (European unity). This was not like 1983, when Mitterrand had faced constraints that had been negotiated before his rise to power, which then imposed themselves on him and forced him to make such a choice. Rather, it was Mitterrand himself who drove a major institutional change at the European level. He well knew – as the 1980s had ensured – that this change would set up an obstacle to any strategy that sought to mediate between public-sector employees' expectations and the expectations of the popular classes.

The French president was thus the leading protagonist in a game that played out at two levels. He acted in Europe to fix rules that particularly concerned budgetary and monetary policy, designed to deeply change the terrain on which projects for political mediation did battle in France. Of course, as a champion of European unity, the president considered France's relationship with Germany a primary concern; but there is also no doubt that the 'constraints' the PS imposed on itself were consistent with the victory of the modernist line within the party. We may also remember that, in 1988, Mitterrand chose the Second Left's leading figure, Michel Rocard, as his prime minister (he would remain in this post for three years). Rocard, moreover, became the PS's first secretary in 1993. This choice certainly was not the result of Mitterrand's personal esteem for Rocard.

It is also highly probable that the recurrent difficulties in the PS's relations with the PCF, as well as the weakening of this latter party, led Mitterrand to try to build social alliances different to those corresponding to the left-wing bloc, in his bid to consolidate his power. The president's strategy can thus also be read as an attempt to block the Parti Communiste definitively from exercising any influence on the action of the 'governmental' left – an action that would henceforth be 'constrained' by European accords. In setting up insurmountable obstacles to the Parti Communiste, Mitterrand consolidated both the Socialists' domination over the left and that of the modernist line within the PS itself. This two-sided achievement allowed him to look towards the political centre in search of new interlocutors.

During the debate over the Maastricht referendum, Mitterrand's strategy brought out another political cleavage that would superimpose itself over the traditional battle between left and right. The supporters of European integration and the neoliberal policies it implied now stood opposed to the defenders of national sovereignty. This new divide fragmented the left; after all, Lutte Ouvrière, the Ligue Communiste Révolutionnaire and the Parti Communiste did battle for the 'No' side, and there were also deep divisions within the Parti Socialiste and the Greens. Most importantly, a gulf opened up between the 'governmental' left and the popular classes – a gulf that only continued to widen over the years that followed. Thus, 58 per cent of blue-collar workers voted 'No' to Maastricht in 1992.[36] They would oppose the ratification of the European Constitutional Treaty in even greater numbers thirteen years later.

In 2005, the complete fracture the European question had produced within the left-wing bloc was fully apparent in the referendum on the European Constitutional Treaty. The Parti Communiste, the Ligue Communiste Révolutionnaire, Lutte Ouvrière and the Parti des Travailleurs campaigned very actively for a 'No' vote, whereas the Parti Socialiste and the Greens backed the ratification of the Treaty. But

---

36   Source: Ifop.

there were divisions within these two parties even deeper than those that had existed at the moment of the Maastricht referendum. Their official positions were established after internal votes by members. The Greens' Inter-Regional National Council, the party's leading body, wrote in 2003 that the Treaty was characterized by

> real but overly limited institutional progress in Part I, a Part II that can be criticized in terms of [its assertion of] the right to work and not the right to a job [and] of the right to life but nothing on the right to contraception and abortion and nothing on European citizenship through residence, a Part III of [neo]liberal orientation that does not suit us and which must be separate from a constitutional text, and a Part IV which defines conditions for its revision [dependent on] unanimity, which would be complicated to put into practice.[37]

In 2004, the French Greens proposed a consultation open to all European ecologists – a proposal rejected by the European Green Party, which was very largely in favour of ratification. There was a lively debate among the French Greens, as the two main figures of political environmentalism in this period took opposite points of view. Daniel Cohn-Bendit was firmly in favour of a treaty he considered a decisive advance towards European unity, whereas José Bové opposed it, judging it 'ultra-[neo]liberal' and 'anti-social'. The debate was settled by a referendum among activists: the 'Yes' side won with 52.7 per cent of the vote, with 42 per cent opting for 'No' and 5.3 per cent abstaining.

The debate on the position to take in the referendum similarly divided the Parti Socialiste. The majority behind First Secretary François Hollande, and the vast majority of local and national-level elected officials, backed ratification, some with unconcealed enthusiasm. Thus, for Dominique Strauss-Kahn – whose opinion perfectly represented the majority of the party – the referendum was reducible to a single question: 'Are we for European integration, yes or no?'[38] The

---

37   'Le 13 février 2005: le référendum des Verts français', in *Archives des Verts français de 1984 à 2010*, at lesverts.fr accessed June 2016.

38   Editorial, 'Référendum européen: les partisans PS du "oui" se mobilisent', *Le Monde*, 12 March 2005

majority of the PS thus followed in Mitterrand's footsteps: if a choice had to be made between Europe and the possibility of a policy that could unite the whole left, not even the slightest hesitation was needed. Yet minority currents – Nouveau Monde and Nouveau Parti Socialiste – opposed ratification. As in the case of the Greens, the debate was settled by an internal referendum where the 'Yes' side won a significant majority (59 per cent), but which also showed that there were much bigger divisions among the party's base than among its elected officials.

Ultimately – and despite the fact that the vast majority of political leaders on both right and left backed ratification – the 'No' side won with 54.7 per cent of the vote. But it should be noted that 'Yes' and 'No' voters did not decide how to vote on the basis of the same variables.

The reasons for the 'Yes' vote were essentially linked to the impact that the referendum result would have on European institutions.[39] Only 8 per cent of voters who supported ratification indicated as a motivation for their vote the belief that it would strengthen 'France's social and economic situation'. The most widespread reasons were that the European Constitutional Treaty was 'indispensable in order to pursue European integration' (39 per cent), because 'I have always been for European integration' (16 per cent); because the Treaty 'strengthens France's place in the [European] Union/in the world' (12 per cent); it 'strengthens the European Union faced with the United States' (11 per cent); and so on. Here it is worth remarking that, even among 'Yes' voters, those who backed ratification because it created 'a real European citizenship' (4 per cent) or because it strengthened 'democracy in Europe/citizen consultation' (4 per cent) were very much in the minority.

Conversely, the motivations for the 'No' vote were mostly linked to the impact the Treaty would have on France's domestic politics and its socioeconomic situation. Thus, 31 per cent of those who had voted 'No' indicated as their motivation the belief that the Treaty would 'have negative effects on the employment situation in France/the outsourcing of French workplaces/job losses'; and 26 per cent gave the reason that 'France's economic situation is too negative/unemployment is too high'.

---

39 The data that follow are taken from 'La Constitution européenne: sondage post-référendum en France', Eurobarometer, European Commission, June 2005.

Only a small minority of those who voted 'No' gave the reason 'I am against Europe/the European project/European integration' (4 per cent), or 'I do not want a European political union/a federal European state/the "United States of Europe"' (2 per cent). Far more rejected the Treaty because it was 'too [neo]liberal in economic terms' (19 per cent) or because it did not propose 'enough of a social Europe' (16 per cent).

In light of these data, we can say that the opinions of 'Yes' voters were not really opposed to those of 'No' voters. This would have been the case if, for example, the pro-Treaty part of the electorate had considered it beneficial for France in socioeconomic terms, or if the part of the electorate opposed to it had simply been averse to the European project. But, more than a frontal opposition, this was a difference over what objectives should be prioritized: for voters who backed ratification, the priority was the Treaty's contribution to the European project, whereas for those opposed to it the most important thing was its consequences for France's economic situation. Thus 52 per cent of those who voted 'Yes' stated that, in making their choice, they had privileged the European dimension (as against 17 per cent of 'No' voters) whereas 47 per cent of 'No' voters declared that they had made their choice by placing a priority on France's socioeconomic situation (as against 11 per cent of those who backed 'Yes').

In a certain sense, the French electorate considered the referendum a choice between two objectives – the fight against unemployment and the pursuit of the European project – that they perceived as incompatible; a choice of the same order as president Mitterrand had had to make back in 1983. But the 'need' to make the choice in 2005 was the product of an institutional dynamic in Europe that the French left, and in particular the Parti Socialiste, had done much to bring about. Thus, through the European strategy upon which it had embarked in the 1980s, and had gone on to pursue with the greatest consistency, the Parti Socialiste was itself at the origin of the fracture in the left-wing bloc.

In the 2005 referendum, there was no trace of the social bloc that had swept Mitterrand to victory in 1981. The Communist electorate almost unanimously voted 'No' (94 per cent), whereas the Socialist and Green electorates were deeply divided. A large share of them did not follow the recommendations issued by the parties' leaders: in each case,

61 per cent of their voters opted for 'No'. If we consider that rejection of the Treaty was principally motivated by fears of the consequences it would have for France's economic situation, and because of its neoliberal dimension, it is far from surprising that 'No' won out among the classes in society that were most under pressure. The most telling vote was doubtless that among blue-collar workers (a 76 per cent 'No' vote), which pointed to the now yawning gulf dividing them from the 'governmental' left. We will return to this in Chapter 3.

Nonetheless, it is important to underline that only 6 per cent of blue-collar workers who voted 'No' gave as their motivation, 'I am against the European project' or 'I do not want a European political union'. Conversely, 60 per cent of them said that they had voted 'No' because the Treaty 'will have negative effects on the employment situation' or because 'France's economic situation is too negative/ unemployment is too high'; 26 per cent rejected the Constitutional Treaty because they thought it did not offer 'enough social Europe' or because it was 'too [neo]liberal in economic terms', because it was 'not democratic enough', or 'out of opposition to the Bolkestein directive' [an EU measure to create a single market in services, controversial for driving competition among workers and a race to the bottom in rights and environmental standards].

It would, therefore, be completely wrong to say that the result of the 2005 referendum was decided by the temptation to retreat into nationalism – a retreat of which the popular classes were supposedly the protagonists. Its rejection was instead driven by the neoliberal character of the Treaty, and the fear of its negative consequences for growth and jobs. It is true, however, that its rejection was essentially the work of the popular classes. While, after the 2004 European elections and before the referendum,[40] the upper and middle classes of French society shared a positive assessment of France's participation in the European Union (71 per cent), only 44 per cent of blue- and white-collar workers did so. At the same time, in 2004, some 65 per cent of blue- and white-collar workers stated that they were proud to be European citizens, and 56 per cent of them wanted French MEPs to defend French *and European* interests in the Brussels and Strasbourg

---

40   Ibid.

parliaments. Only 32 per cent of them called on MEPs to defend French interests alone.

Lastly, in 2004, some 60 per cent of blue- and white-collar workers 'rejected the exclusion of those hailing from other EU countries from French social security, and 54 per cent agreed with the latter being granted the right to vote in local elections'.[41]

We can see, then, that a new political divide was superimposed upon the familiar battle between left and right. This new split, which set the popular classes in opposition to the middle and upper classes, did not – back then, at least – correspond to an opposition between 'pro-Europeans' and 'nationalists'. Rather, it was essentially based on the different perception of the impact that a neoliberal integration of Europe would have on socioeconomic conditions in France. Behind the fear – widespread among the popular classes – of the 'socioeconomic consequences of European integration, we find a more diffuse social anxiety regarding the globalized economy, liberalization and the resulting job precarity. This anxiety moreover goes hand-in-hand with the individualization of employment conditions and the isolation it produces'.[42]

HOLLANDE'S PRESIDENCY

Hollande's presidency was the end point of a historical process with much deeper roots. Modernist ideology – rejecting not just Marxism but any reading of social and economic dynamics in terms of conflict – had already been present in some currents of the PS in the 1970s, and in effect much earlier than that. But the French electoral system's majoritarian character had forced the Socialist leaders of the day to show 'flexibility' in their negotiations with a Parti Communiste so powerful as to represent an unavoidable stepping-stone towards power. This situation evolved over subsequent years, continually in connection with support for the European project. In the two parties' negotiations over the *programme commun de gouvernement* (joint manifesto), the PS constantly considered European integration a primary objective

41   Ibid.
42   Ibid.

that underpinned all of its activity. We have emphasized the consistency of this position; it dates back a long way, even to before World War II, to a modernism that saw Europe as a factor that would drive modernization, and international competition as a fundamental factor in injecting dynamism into France's productive base.

The turn to austerity, the Maastricht referendum, and the vote on the draft European Constitution represent so many phases in a shift that had three major effects. These were: a) the weakening of the Socialists' Communist ally, and the consolidation of the PS's own hegemony over the left; b) the ideological alignment of PS representatives to the positions of the Second Left or, more generally, to those of 'reformists' who were more or less faithful heirs to modernism; and c) the distancing of the PS from the popular classes at its base. This was far from fortuitous or necessary, and it resembled an expulsion: the PS actively took part in the construction of the European constraints that then 'compelled it', 'out of economic realism', first to abandon any prospect of responding to mass unemployment, and then to drive the neoliberal transformation of the French model.

Hollande's term as president was the outcome of this trajectory. It was an end-point, firstly because all of his actions followed one single orientation. Free of allies to its left for the first time in its history, the PS conformed to the European directives it was itself secretly negotiating, and introduced neoliberal reforms to the heart of the French model, by attacking the labour code. Hollande's term as president was also the outcome – and culmination – of the party's electoral trajectory, with the collapse in support for the PS's actions. In establishing its ideological domination over the PS, the Second Left deliberately sabotaged the left-wing bloc; but, despite the fine advice coming from Terra Nova, it has yet to identify a social base for its own project.

Thus, for almost forty years, the Socialists have won elections with promises delivered to a left-wing bloc that, logically enough, they do not then keep once in power. Coming at the end of this trajectory, Hollande paid the price for almost four decades of let-downs. But such a violent collapse in the PS's electoral and political support has naturally sparked a reaction by the party in its search for an exit route. And it thinks it has found one in the bourgeois bloc.

CHAPTER 3

The Bourgeois Bloc: A New Hegemonic Bloc?

The fracturing of the left-wing bloc dates back to the 'turn to austerity' (*tournant de la rigueur*). Since that era the Parti Socialiste has searched in vain for the social base appropriate to the 'modernist' strategy that is widely dominant among its cadres and leaders. Thus, we need to turn back to the early 1980s in order to give an account of a quest that has ultimately translated into the gradual emergence of an unprecedented political project. This project implies profound change in the cleavages structuring French politics, and it coincides with the formation of a new social alliance: the bourgeois bloc.

THE IDEOLOGICAL VICTORY OF MODERNISM AND EUROPEAN INTEGRATION: THE END OF THE LEFT-WING BLOC

We have referred to the left-wing bloc that existed in the 1970s and 1980s – the coalition of social groups that considered that their interests were represented by the political alliance of left-wing parties, particularly the PS and PCF. It was never homogenous either in its sociology (which is no surprise; blocs are a priori heterogenous, since they result from the combination of diverse social groups) or in its aspirations (which was, conversely, more problematic from the perspective of the bloc's stability). This lack of homogeneity can also be identified in the different political formations on the left. If the PCF more strongly represented the bloc's blue-collar component, the PS was very diverse, embodying the interests of service workers (whose aspirations were similar to those of industrial workers) as well as the educated middle classes, who had more 'qualitative' demands.[1]

---

1   See Bruno Amable, Elvire Guillaud and Stefano Palombarini, *L'Économie politique du néolibéralisme. Le cas de la France et de l'Italie* (Paris: éd. Rue d'Ulm, 2012); Bruno Amable,

The left's political project, from the joint manifesto of the 1970s to Mitterrand's *110 Proposals for France* in 1981, expressed a compromise between potentially divergent aspirations. Low-income social groups placed a great deal of hope in policies that would increase wages, cut unemployment, consolidate and extend the welfare state, and so on. Better-off social groups were more prone to demands that concerned cultural openness and civil rights, and they were also distrustful of state intervention. From the economic point of view, they above all hoped that the Socialist government would drive a policy that would renew France's institutions and the structures organising its economy, in line with the modernist aspirations of the post-war period. For reasons of political realism, until the left's arrival in power in 1981 its programme was above all orientated towards this first type of expectation. The groups that identified with the modernist project were in the minority among the left's whole social bloc, and indeed in the political formations that corresponded to it.

The left's arrival in power thus implied a need to satisfy the most immediate quantitative expectations. Indeed, the first decisions by the left-wing coalition government in 1981 were situated in this perspective; a 10 per cent increase in the minimum wage and a 25 per cent rise in family and old-age benefits; the hiring of 55,000 civil servants; support for the construction of social housing; cutting the pension age to sixty; a fifth week of paid holidays. This was accompanied by other measures that aimed to transform the structures of the economy, including the nationalization of banks and a large share of industry, and restrictions on the use of temporary and interim contracts.

The assessment that both the press and the scholarly literature make of the government's economic policy, starting in 1981, is usually negative. It is true that even if France's economic kick-start programme managed to avert recession and temporarily contain unemployment, it did not manage to revive the economy. Moreover, the path chosen in order to kick-start the economy ran against the positions the other OECD countries had taken faced with recession (here following the United States), which caused a major foreign trade imbalance. We can

Structural Crisis and Institutional Change in Modern Capitalism: French Capitalism in Transition (Oxford, Oxford University Press, 2017).

nonetheless note that Reagan's and Thatcher's respective economic policy initiatives themselves gave rise to a similar or even larger deepening of the foreign trade deficit, not to mention the effects on unemployment; yet no one concluded that it was necessary to set a new course for economic policy – quite the opposite.[2] Moreover, the discussions on economic matters during the drafting of the joint manifesto and the *110 Proposals* were not limited to a choice between 'Keynesian deficit' and 'austerity'. Rather, they entailed a transformation of the productive model, which would proceed by way of a medium- or long-term action going far beyond a kick-start programme designed to stimulate economic activity in the short term. Coming just a few months after the first of the *110 Proposals* were implemented, the 'turn to austerity' denied the continuation of the left's economic experiment: it quite simply consisted of aligning both short- and long-term French economic policy to the dominant choices of the times, which pointed in the direction of neoliberalization.

However, as we emphasized in Chapter 2, the first phase of Mitterrand's presidency was not characterized by the search for 'technical' solutions to economic problems, but rather by an outright ideological battle. For the modernist component of the Parti Socialiste, the time had come to apply a programme that had long been in gestation, and to do so by exploiting all the opportunities that the economic situation might offer to advance a so-called 'realistic' discourse. The latter was designed finally to bury the joint manifesto, marginalize the Parti Communiste, and prioritize neoliberal structural reforms. This would also sacrifice the expectations of a substantial part of the left-wing bloc, in particular the working class, and more generally the lowest-income groups in French society.[3]

This battle began as soon as the left took power – indeed, it would be wrong to say that the government's economic policy orientation changed abruptly in 1983. Fonteneau and Muet emphasize that the

---

2   See Amable, *Structural Crisis and Institutional Change*.

3   We can note that, in the late 1970s and early 1980s, demands for a left-wing economic policy (nationalizations, more public services even at the cost of tax rises, opposition to austerity) were particularly supported by the youngest. Amable, *Structural Crisis and Institutional Change*.

genuinely expansionist phase in Socialist policy – which placed a priority on cutting unemployment – had already ended in June 1982.[4] The measures that accompanied the devaluation of the franc announced a change of course that became explicit in March 1983, at the moment of a turn to austerity that had been in the air for several months. The then economy minister, Jacques Delors, considered that the market for goods was affected by excess demand, which he quantified at 2 per cent of GDP; eliminating this imbalance (as well as the inflation and the trade deficit it produced) now replaced the fight against unemployment among the government's priorities.

But the 1 per cent rise in income tax, the tax hikes applied to tobacco and alcohol, the increase in the charges for public services, and the 7 billion franc cut in planned public spending signalled not just a change of economic policy priorities. Rather, the choice to make reducing the trade deficit a higher priority than cutting unemployment corresponded to a change in the internal dynamics of the PS. The consequence of this was a revision of its alliance strategy, and ultimately a change in the left's electoral base.

The decision was therefore to keep the franc within the European Monetary System. This implied concentrating government action on the fight against inflation and deficits – a course that was chosen in preference to exiting the EMS in order to allow the pursuit of the economic policy that had been embarked upon in 1981. The question to which Mitterrand responded in making this choice was above all a political one: Was it necessary to satisfy the expectations of the social groups making up the left's electoral base, which had brought it to victory, or – by reaffirming France's presence in the EMS – to carry out the austerity measures the large majority of these same social groups had rejected in 1981?

The answer did not seem obvious, for there were violent conflicts within the PS regarding the *political* perspectives for Mitterrand's term. The Parti Socialiste was divided into two rival camps. Yet they did battle with the greatest of discretion – for each of them knew that the final choice would come from the president, and thus its

---

4   Alain Fonteneau and Pierre-Alain Muet, *La Gauche face à la crise* (Paris: Presses de Sciences Po, 1985).

task was to convince him that its own preferred option was the most appropriate.

The fight thus played out rather more in the corridors of the Élysée Palace than in the court of public opinion. The modernists ended up securing a definitive victory. Mitterrand was well aware that his decision was far from just a matter of the particular conjuncture. After all, keeping the franc within the EMS entailed both a lasting end to demand-boosting policies and the implementation of austerity policies with social and political consequences that all the participants in the intra-PS clash – on both the winning and losing sides – had factored into their respective arguments. Economic strategy henceforth consisted of driving a supply-side policy aimed at creating an environment favourable to private investment.[5] Wage restraint played a decisive role within this framework. In his *Verbatim*, Jacques Attali confirms that Mitterrand was conscious of the profound and lasting implications of the turn to austerity: 'I am split between two ambitions: European integration and social justice. The EMS is necessary to succeed on the first count and limits my freedom [of action] for the second.'[6]

As we stressed in Chapter 2, there was in fact nothing surprising in Mitterrand's choice: European integration was one of the PS's red lines in the negotiations that had led to the Union de la Gauche in the 1970s. We may question the seriousness of the concessions the joint manifesto made to the PCF on the question of nationalizations, as well as the sincerity of the many calls for a rupture with capitalism. Indeed, these could each be interpreted as cases of adopting a position for tactical reasons – functional both to the battle for hegemony within the left-wing coalition, fought between Socialists and Communists, and the fight for the leadership of the PS itself. But there is no doubt that, from the 1970s onwards, the PS made a major strategic choice in favour of taking part in European integration. It is thus unsurprising that, when it had to choose between the EMS and an economic policy that conformed to the expectations of the left-wing bloc, Mitterrand

---

5   Frédéric Lordon, *Les Quadratures de la politique économique* (Paris: Albin Michel, 1997).

6   Jacques Attali, *Verbatim I* (Paris: Fayard, 1993), p. 399.

prioritized the former. Although, in the 1970s, they had been in the minority – indeed on the retreat within the party – the modernists scored a decisive success for their struggle by carving European unity in stone as a non-negotiable goal of Socialist strategy.

If the outcome of this fight was, within certain limits, decided in advance, the battle that broke out in the Parti Socialiste after it took power was no less hard-fought for that. The opponents of the most important left-wing reforms at the beginning of Mitterrand's term profited from the relative failure of the 1981 policy to kick-start the economy, and above all from the worsening trade deficit, to drama-tize the situation and insist on a change of course. In November 1981, Jacques Delors publicly called for a 'pause' in the reforms, just a few weeks after the first measures contained in François Mitterrand's *110 Proposals for France* had been enacted.[7] The modernists' victory was both complete and unambiguous. It was so total that the dominant interpretation of the 1983 turn would mask its political dimension. It was instead characterized as a return to supposed 'economic realism', or the consequence of the need to put in place a supply-side policy, compelled by external constraints.

This interpretation has been preponderant not only in the media but also in economic policy literature. According to this point of view, the (relative) failure of the Keynesian strategy to kick-start growth implied the lasting abandonment of any *dirigiste* management of demand, and the reorientation of economic policy towards the quest for competitiveness and the promotion of the enterprise as an actor strategically decisive for growth. This analysis in the media and in scholarship was the same as that of major actors in French politics like Michel Rocard and Jacques Delors, who had an obvious tactical inter-est in presenting their strategy as the only possible one. The political choice Mitterrand had made thus represented a defeat for left-wing social and economic policy; the electoral loss in 1986 was the logical

---

7   In his memoir, Jacques Delors admits that the use of the word 'pause' was deliberate here. It echoed the use of this same word by the Socialist prime minister in 1937, which the left-wing electorate interpreted as the beginning of the end for France's first Popular Front government. Delors's intention in using this word in 1981 was to produce a 'psychological electric shock' on the left. Jacques Delors, *Mémoires* (Paris: Plon, 2004), p. 148.

consequence of disappointing the expectations of a large fraction of the social bloc that had brought the left to power in 1986.[8] The line of economic orthodoxy – constantly presented as a choice in favour of European integration – was followed more or less rigorously by all the left-wing governments that followed (1988–93, 1997–2002, 2012–17), with the same disastrous electoral consequences. The fraction of the left-wing bloc sacrificed by Socialist strategy did not limit itself to signalling its discontent at the ballot box. Already during Mitterrand's second term (1988–95), there were numerous cases of social opposition to the government's actions coming from within the left's own base. By way of examples we could mention the tax administration employees' strike in 1989 (which forced the Finance Ministry to grant them a special bonus), or the great nurses' protests of 1991, during the final months of the Rocard government. The 1993 parliamentary elections were catastrophic for the PS, which obtained only 20 per cent of the vote, and forced Mitterrand into a second *cohabitation* with a prime minister from the right.

Socialist officialdom was well aware of the contradiction between the expectations of a major part of their base and an economic policy that only extended Raymond Barre's own actions. As the PS's first secretary in 1983, Lionel Jospin had presented the turn to austerity as a 'parenthesis' – a temporary deviation from a left-wing trajectory – which implied that the new course of economic policy would ultimately be reversed.[9] Yet the architects of the turn, Delors first among them, did not share this view: for them, the return to supposed 'economic realism' was a permanent change in economic policy, indeed in the 'proper' direction.[10]

The rhetoric about a 'parenthesis' masked the crushing ideological and political victory the modernists had won within the PS. Yet – even now – no social bloc able to assure electoral victory corresponds to the

---

8   Liêm Hoang Ngoc, *Refermons la parenthèse libérale!* (Paris: La Dispute, 2005).

9   Lionel Jospin considers his government's social and economic policy (in its spell in office from 1997 to 2002) as a rupture with the turn made in 1983. This is only partly true. See Henri Sterdyniak, 'Le gouvernement Jospin (1997–2002): un social-libéralisme français?', in *Les Politiques économiques de la gauche en France (1936–2002)*, papers from the conference hosted by the Fondation Gabriel-Péri (Pantin: Fondation Gabriel-Péri, 2012).

10   Delors, *Mémoires*, p. 161.

dominant line within the party. There has been no lack of attempts to build new social alliances; but, from 1981 until Hollande's victory in the 2012 presidential election, the PS constantly sought the support of the left-wing bloc in its election campaigns. To acknowledge that the PS is today very widely perceived as a party of let-downs is no moral reproach; rather, it is explained by the ambition to govern prevalent in a party that has yet to find the social bedrock for its political strategy.

TRANSFORMATIONS IN THE EMPLOYMENT RELATION AT THE HEART OF CAPITALISM'S EVOLUTIONS

The 1980s – the years that saw the victory of the modernist line within the Parti Socialiste – were characterized by profound changes within European capitalism, all working in the direction of the (neo)liberal model. Yet, in France as in the European countries most distant from liberal capitalism, there was no explicit rupture or sudden swing towards new ways of organizing capitalism. Rather, there has been a gradual slide – one that began over thirty years ago and still today is not fully complete.

The institutional changes in a particular domain have consequences in other fields, through the interplay of institutional complementarities. Thus, in numerous European countries, privatizations have challenged the status of workers employed by public companies. This has helped weaken macro-corporatism (the centralized management of labour–capital relations) and favoured the spread of micro-corporatism (the management of employer–employee relations at the workplace level). This micro-corporatism is more in accordance with the neoliberal model of capitalism.

Similarly, in increasing the pressure for strong short-term yields, the financialization of the economy has made it more difficult to provide wage-earners with the effective guarantee of a certain measure of job security. The expansion of the financial markets has also led to competition between the provision of private (insurance) services and public social protection systems – central elements of the sociopolitical compromises on which continental European and social-democratic capitalisms are grounded.

At the beginning of the twenty-first century, the institutions of employment relations are at the centre of change. They have undergone major transformations in many countries, gradually (and to varying degrees) orientating these institutions towards the neoliberal model. It is no accident that, in France's gradual transition towards the neoliberal model, the transformation of these institutions has come last: they were the essential element of the social compromises that underpinned the old modes of economic organization.[11] More than a generalized flexibilization of the labour market and a complete dismantling of social protection – one challenging the protection mechanisms indispensable to the sociopolitical compromises on which many continental European capitalisms still base themselves – what has instead been seen in Europe is a partial liberalization, affecting those at the margins more than the core workforce.

Regulationist authors thought that they could identify the main elements of a post-Fordist employment relation in certain characteristics of Asian capitalism. Picking up on employment relations at Toyota, it was supposed that this could establish a compromise between 'job stability, malleable tasks and a production sufficiently diversified that it would allow workers to be redeployed within the company according to the fortunes of different markets, supposed to be counter-cyclical'.[12] But this model has not spread across the Japanese economy, still less to developed economies as a whole. External flexibility has gradually imposed itself as the dominant theme of the transformation of the employment relation, supposed to guarantee rapid and efficient adjustments of the workforce in favour of the most efficient firms and sectors. 'External flexibility ... should be conjugated with all elements of the employment relation, the salary, the form of social coverage, the duration of work, and so on.'[13] The hypothesis here is that technological change relies on innovations that do so much to change the structure of industry that the destruction of jobs is simultaneously both a consequence and a

---

11   See Amable, Guillaud and Palombarini, *L'Économie politique du néolibéralisme*.

12   Robert Boyer, 'L'hétérogénéité des relations salariales contemporaines et ses conséquences', intervention at the conference on 'Les sciences sociales en mutation', Paris, 3–6 May 2006, p. 2.

13   Ibid.

condition of productivity gains. In these circumstances, the institutions imagined to put the brakes on such a destruction of jobs are supposed to have a similar effect in slowing growth.

Therefore, the question is: What social alliance could sustain a relation to waged employment considerably more flexibilized and segmented than that which existed in the period following the 1970s crisis? It is obvious that, in non-neoliberal models of capitalism, there is no social bloc large and stable enough to sustain a complete liberalization of the whole employment relationship (including in its social-protection dimensions).[14] This is why attempts at 'reform' have sought a bloc that would accommodate to partial changes.

In some countries there has been an effort to preserve the traditional employment relationship for the core workforce – composed of skilled workers employed in export industries – while flexibilizing it in service industries or those protected from international competition. We thus observe a growing segmentation – albeit one that varies depending on the country – between the core and the periphery of the workforce, with employment relations that conserve all or, most often, part of the 'good' properties of stability (job security, gradually rising wages), reserved to wage-earners useful to the stability and development of specific firm competences; whereas what is proposed for the others is a more precarious employment relationship.

This reform strategy[15] was notably adopted in Germany in order to push down unemployment and the resulting pressure in terms of

14   By way of example, one poll (Harris Interactive for the CGT, September 2012) of support for possible measures to combat unemployment showed that 61 per cent of those surveyed opposed the flexibilization of employment relations through a weakening of job-protection legislation, while 37 per cent were in favour. We find a similar split of opinion in the (lack of) support for proposals for a 'single employment contract'. Bruno Amable, 'Who Wants the Contrat de Travail Unique? Social Support for Labor Market Flexibilization in France', *Industrial Relations* 53: 4 (2014). Indeed, a series of attempts at 'reforms' to employment law (CPE, Loi Travail) and to social protection (the Juppé reform, Sarkozy's pension reforms) over the span of twenty years have given rise to large strike movements.

15   This phenomenon has especially been studied by the numerous political scientists who have discovered – fifteen years late, but with boundless enthusiasm – the insider-outsider model developed by certain economists. Taking not the slightest critical distance, they have adopted the most caricatural conclusions that one could draw from this model regarding the 'wicked' insiders whose high level of protections is supposedly responsible for the outsiders' woes.

financing social protection, as well as to reduce labour costs in service industries – and, as a consequence, total production costs in export industries that directly or indirectly drew on these services.[16] Moreover, flexibilization of labour around the edges also brings pressure for 'wage moderation' (in reality meaning stagnation in real wages) for workers in core industries. The champions of these reforms may not necessarily have anticipated it, but these transformations have sparked an increase in conflict, showing the contradictions of the new type of employment relation: fiscal austerity has led to very tight limits on wage rises in public services; privatizations have removed civil servants' status and undermined employment conditions in numerous previously public services; growing segmentation has increased the disorganized diversity of demands – and so on.

The new forms of employment relation thus seem less appropriate for accomplishing what the Fordist one could do: namely, to provide the means for a gradual rise in effective demand by way of productivity gains. The segmentation of the labour market brings rising inequality, and the choice to compete on the grounds of cost-competitiveness increases the imbalance in the share of income between labour and capital. A number of works, notably Thomas Piketty's worldwide bestseller, have demonstrated the degree to which inequalities have soared since the early 1980s.[17] In many countries, wages have consistently risen at a slower rate than productivity. The most flagrant such example is the United States, but this phenomenon is present, again to different degrees, across all industrialized countries. We are almost rediscovering some of the characteristics of pre-Fordist regulation by competition.

The development of atypical forms of employment around the edges of the waged workforce has brought up old debates on the segmentation of the labour market and social protection. These developments increase inequalities – even more so given that social-protection systems have tended to become less generous, particularly

---

16 Wolfgang Streeck, *Re-Forming Capitalism. Institutional Change in the German Political Economy* (Oxford/New York: Oxford University Press, 2009).

17 Thomas Piketty, *Capital in the Twenty-First Century* (Cambridge, MA: Harvard University Press, 2014).

insofar as unemployment compensation is ever more linked to the efforts made to seek insertion into the labour market (activation). The question of the sociopolitical stability of these transformed economies can thus be posed in the more or less short term. Contrary to the conclusions drawn by Martin and Swank,[18] optimistic that macro-corporatist systems will be able to limit inequalities of income and status, the evolution towards a more unequal and competition-based employment relationship has also affected the Nordic countries, and Sweden in particular.[19] The countries that seem most to have escaped the dynamic of the 'dualization' of the labour market are those where employment protections are weak for everyone (Switzerland and Denmark), and where the homogenization of the employment relationship takes the form of a levelling-down.[20] This lessens the pressures for deregulation taken at the bosses' own initiative.

This leaves open the question of what social alliance is likely to support such transformations. This problem is posed in different terms in each country, as they have different socioeconomic structures. The definition of sociopolitical groups, their relative importance, and their expectations also necessarily differ. If the hard core of neoliberalism is probably very similar from one country to the next (the self-employed, top managers, company directors, and so on), it is, without doubt, nowhere a social majority.[21] The adoption of neoliberal reforms – even partially – thus demands a mediation strategy that is able to aggregate a variety of social groups around this hard core, thus constituting a dominant social bloc.

On this last point, the comparison between France and Italy explored by Amable, Guillaud and Palombarini and by Amable and Palombarini has revealed the existence of a 'bourgeois bloc' centred

---

18   Cathie Jo Martin and Duane Swank, *The Political Construction of Business Interests: Coordination, Growth and Equality* (Oxford: Oxford University Press, 2012).

19   Gerhard Schnyder, 'Like a Phoenix from the Ashes? Reassessing the Transformation of the Swedish Political Economy since the 1970s', *Journal of European Public Policy* 19: 8 (2012).

20   Patrick Emmenegger, *The Power to Dismiss: Trade Unions and the Regulation of Job Security in Western Europe* (Oxford: Oxford University Press, 2015).

21   See the comparative analysis covering both France and Italy in Amable, Guillaud and Palombarini, *L'Économie politique du néolibéralisme*.

on the highly educated middle and upper classes.[22] This bloc has the potential to become a dominant bloc, and is, according to all evidence, the social alliance on which the coalitions in power in each of these two countries have based their political and institutional strategies.

THE DIFFICULT EMERGENCE OF A BOURGEOIS BLOC

A social bloc is always the result of action by political forces. They propose a set of economic and structural policies appropriate to satisfying different social groups. The formation, and indeed the rupturing, of a bloc cannot be analysed independently of the political strategies linked to the blocs in question. There is no unidirectional relation of cause and effect in which social expectations (which are not inherently compatible or incompatible) are then expressed in political action; the role of the latter is not simply to adapt to changing expectations in a more or less passive way. A social bloc is the product of a political project, and its break-up can be explained in terms of the emergence of alternative projects. The rupture in the left-wing bloc in France has largely been the consequence of the 'governmental' left's political actions. Similarly, while the emergence of a bourgeois bloc does, without doubt, correspond to concordances between the expectations of the groups called on to compose it, this is also a concordance organized and given structure by a political strategy.

The bourgeois bloc and the political forces corresponding to it thus need to be analysed as conjoined phenomena. These political forces' shared horizon is the neoliberal reform of French capitalism; but the social expectations linked to neoliberal reforms are a factor for political crisis in France, since they fracture the old social blocs. The Cevipof has put together an 'index of economic liberalism' based on three questions: 'Should we give more trust to businesses and give them more freedom?' 'Should we give businesses more freedom to fire workers?', and 'Should we reduce the number of civil servants?'.[23]

---

22   Ibid.; Bruno Amable and Stefano Palombarini, 'The Bloc Bourgeois in France and Italy', in Hideko Magara, ed., *Economic Crises and Policy Regimes: The Dynamics of Policy Innovation and Paradigmatic Change* (Cheltenham: Edward Elgar, 2014).

23   Luc Rouban, 'Existe-t-il un électorat social-libéral?', *L'enquête électorale française: comprendre 2017*, wave 3, Cevipof at enef.fr/les-notes, accessed June 2017.

Considering 'liberal' those respondents who answer 'yes' to at least two questions, it then compared this index with the vote in the regional elections of 2015. The result was that 'liberals' are present to varying degrees in all parties' electoral base: they represent 53 per cent of voters for the republican right, 34 per cent of FN voters, and 19 per cent of voters who backed a left-wing list. 'Liberals' are thus not only in the minority (around a third of the electorate), but also dispersed.

For some time, the neoliberal reform of French capitalism advanced in disguised form, attacking institutions that might have seemed peripheral to the old social compromises. But at the moment when the 'reform' process turned to target the institutions of the labour market – the keystone of a social model that it sought to bury – the constitution of a social bloc in support of reforms became a necessity if they were to succeed. In terms of the expectations expressed by voters, this bloc appeared as a minority, albeit a sizeable one; it thus posed itself the problem of how it could expand by establishing alliances.

Nonetheless, the most immediate obstacle to the composition of such a bloc is the traditional structuring of the 'supply' side of the political exchange, since the supporters of neoliberal reforms are dispersed. Thus, the first task is to unite them. In this sense, the European integration process plays a decisive political role – on the one hand, because the 'necessary reforms' the European institutions call for work exactly in the direction of the neoliberal model; on the other hand, because the objective of European unification can be presented as something that transcends the stakes of national politics, and thus serve as a lever for restructuring the national political 'supply'. Jacques Delors was the precursor of such a strategy: his ambition to rally 'wise men from all sides' to give their approval to austerity policies was heralded as functional to the European project – and it constituted the first politically significant challenge to the traditional left–right divide.[24]

We can, moreover, reinterpret in this same light Mitterrand's strategy through the 1980s aimed at encouraging the rise of the Front National. The most widespread interpretation of this strategy attaches it to the goal of dividing, and thus weakening, the right. This is doubtless

---

24 Expression used in Philippe Alexandre and Jacques Delors, *En sortir ou pas* (Paris: Grasset, 1983), p. 28.

true. But there may have been another, connected objective, making space for further political recompositions, with a view to a break with, and the decline of, the Parti Communiste. That is, to divide the right and push the most radical fraction of its electorate into the arms of the Front National would also open up the possibility for the Parti Socialiste to identify new allies coming from the 'moderate' right. The choice of a proportional electoral system for the 1986 parliamentary elections (allowing the election of 35 Front National MPs), but also the appointment of Michel Rocard as prime minister in 1988, can thus be interpreted as an attempt to recompose the political landscape. In 1993 Michel Rocard openly called for such a recomposition, making an appeal for a political 'big bang'. Issued in Montlouis-sur-Loire on 17 February that year, this call was addressed 'to all that environmentalism has in terms of reformers, to all that centrism has in terms of loyalists to a social tradition, to all that communism has that is truly for renewal, to all that the forces of human rights today have in terms of active militants'.[25]

At the time, this strategy failed. Delors's refusal to stand in the 1995 presidential election, as described in the previous chapter, doomed it to defeat. However, what did live on was the project of restructuring the political supply around a 'Europeanist' pole that supported neoliberal reforms. And, in 2007, a presidential candidate was indeed found, willing and available to champion it explicitly. François Bayrou campaigned on three themes: support for European integration and the 'necessary' reforms it implied; the will to transcend a left–right divide deemed obsolete; denunciation of the other candidates' 'unrealistic' proposals and the defence of a policy of austerity, given the need to concentrate the few available resources on cutting taxes on business. On this basis, Bayrou secured a remarkable result – 18.6 per cent in the first round. This also demonstrated that building a bourgeois bloc was now politically imaginable – on condition, at least, that one of the two main parties rallied to such a project.

An electoral survey in 1988 asked voters which of the following possible coalitions they would prefer in government: PS+PCF, the

---

25   Cited in 'Michel Rocard: avec les centristes et les écolos', L'Humanité, 19 February 1993.

PS alone, PS+centrists, UDF+RPR, UDF+RPR+FN, or PS+UDF+ RPR.[26] An analysis of voters' responses shows that hopes placed in a future alliance between Socialists and centrists were linked to a liberal, non-interventionist economic policy.[27] The preference for this type of alliance was associated with progressive aspirations on so-called 'cultural issues' (lack of hostility to immigrants, defence of civil liberties), but not to demands for a 'left-wing' economic policy. Sociologically speaking, these coalition preferences and the corresponding expectations were rooted in layers of the population with middle-to-upper incomes and education levels. We thus see the emergence of a schema that would serve as a reference point for countless political-science analyses based on 'dealignment' and 'modernization', whose most caricatural outcome was the Terra Nova publication discussed in Chapter 1, which came out before the 2012 presidential election. Yet this reading of the results of the 1988 survey – which yields a relatively 'moderate' image of the expectations of what might constitute the bourgeois bloc – too narrowly reflects the question posed. For the alternatives that the pollster specified presuppose a vision of the PS-centrist alliance as a middle course between traditional left and right. But a closer analysis indicates that the bourgeois bloc is far from 'moderate' in all its expectations.

The sociological profile of this bloc in formation was clearly apparent in the 2005 referendum on the draft European Constitution. By its very nature, this vote made it possible to anticipate how social alliances would be restructured if traditional political attachments were really breaking up, and the European question was becoming the foundational axis of France's political 'supply'. It was also telling because of the high turnout (69 per cent of eligible voters). According to pollsters, the 'Yes' camp rallied 60 to 65 per cent of the liberal professions and intellectuals and 67 per cent of managers, whereas 'No' was easily in the majority among farmers (70 per cent) and both white-collar (60 to 67 per cent) and blue-collar (71 to 81 per cent) workers.[28] It thus appears

---

26   Cevipof post-electoral study, *Banque de Données socio-Politiques CIDSP*, 1988.

27   Amable, *Structural Crisis and Institutional Change*.

28   Gaëtane Ricard-Nihoul, 'Le "non" français du 29 mai 2005: comprendre, agir', *Notre Europe, Études et Recherches* 44 (October 2005), citing the surveys by CSA, Ipsos and Sofres.

that the transcendence of the left–right divide implies – contrary to what the usual political rhetoric indicates – the establishment of a new social alliance very clearly based on class. The popular-class categories, some fractions of which were part of the right-wing bloc (and not just the left-wing one), are, as a whole, excluded from the bourgeois bloc. At the same time, support for European integration brings together the 'bourgeois' classes which the left–right cleavage divides (by way of example, intellectual professions, traditionally on the left, voted en masse for 'Yes' in the referendum – but so did private-sector managers, strongly anchored to the right).

The bourgeois bloc is thus, it seems, the outcome of the modernist strategy now hegemonic within the Parti Socialiste. This is the alliance André Gauron described in his discussion of the modernists' failure until 1981:

> [T]heir defeat is first of all the consequence of their refusal to accept French society such as it is, to take it into the embrace of the state in order to guide its evolution. The modernists have remained 'Mendé-sists' refusing to count the Communist votes, which ultimately means [refusing] to take into account the expectations of working-class France. They have constructed a 'modern' salariat of their own, of technicians, managers, tertiary employees, the 'white collar'; they have equipped themselves with new social movements, feminists, auton-omists, environmentalists … who mobilize this 'modern' salariat. Blue-collar France, the working 'class', remains foreign to them, except when they see it as exclusively foreign, that is, [made up of] immi-grants. Hence the economic crisis … is incomprehensible to them.[29]

If we pick up on the analysis in terms of latent classes as pre-sented by Amable, Guillaud and Palombarini, we can more accurately sketch out a profile of the bourgeois bloc.[30] This analysis breaks

---

29 André Gauron, *Années de rêves, Années de crises (1970–1981). Histoire économique et sociale de la Ve République*, vol. II (Paris: La Découverte, 1988), p. 288.

30 Latent classes are aspects of a statistical model which groups individuals into classes in terms of similar characteristics they share. Here, classes are determined on the basis of answers to questions about their public policy outlook. Amable, Guillaud and Palomba-rini, *L'Économie politique du néolibéralisme*.

down the French electorate into homogenous classes on the basis of their expressed expectations. Several of these classes are liable to be integrated into the new social alliance. The class that expresses the expectations most consistent with the project of the bourgeois bloc closely corresponds to the 'social-liberals' identified by the Cevipof study cited above.[31] This is an urban class (39 per cent of its members live in big cities), well-off in economic terms, largely made up of managers (49 per cent of the total), which sees social inequalities and the education and training of young people as priority issues. This class, which favours neoliberal reforms even if it finds them too fast-paced, represented 9 per cent of the electorate in 2012. Given the small size of this social group, the construction of a bourgeois bloc demands that it reach out to include others.

For the moment, the left–right cleavage separates 'social-liberals' (the large majority of whom, in our analysis, position themselves on the centre-left) from another bourgeois class. Also economically well-off, this second class counted for 13 per cent of the electorate in 2012, and largely considered itself to be on the moderate right. This second class is sociologically similar to the first, with a large proportion of top managers, business leaders and the self-employed (42 per cent of this class) and high education levels (67 per cent have at least a *diplôme du second degré*, similar to UK A-levels). This second class also considers the education and training of young people to be a priority objective. Like the first, it voted en masse for 'Yes' in the referendum on the European Constitution. Differences emerge mainly in terms of the pace of reforms (this second class would prefer that they came faster), privatizations (65 per cent of this second class look upon them favourably, while the 'social-liberals' take a mainly negative view), and immigration, a theme on which the first class takes a much more open attitude than the second.

Overall, a compromise between these two classes – founded on the pursuit of European integration and the employment of public resources to favour the education and training of young people and keeping businesses competitive – seems entirely possible. The main

---

31 Rouban, 'Existe-t-il un électorat social-libéral?'

obstacle remains their very different self-positioning on the left–right axis; but if the political 'supply' were restructured around the European question, these two classes would find, rather spontaneously, that they are allies.

The transcendence of the left–right divide and the establishment of a pro-European alliance would also correspond to a choice to build a sociological unity around the educated, well-off classes on the basis of shared neoliberal positions on economic matters. This new compromise would have the advantage of pursuing the choice – more or less implicitly made by the parties in power thus far – in favour of European integration and structural reforms. But, rather inconveniently, the new alliance would unite less than a quarter of the electorate (its components representing 9 and 13 per cent of voters, respectively).

Nonetheless, we should add two qualifications, so that we can gauge the importance of this problem in more relative terms. The first concerns the fact that our analysis regards all citizens as eligible to vote. But the mass – and growing – abstention among the popular classes visible in recent contests, especially among blue-collar workers and white-collar employees, necessarily increases the bourgeois classes' own electoral weight. A quarter of the electorate may translate into a far higher percentage of the vote if around 60 per cent of the popular classes continue to abstain. That said, it is impossible to know whether this disposition towards electoral exit will remain dominant among the popular classes, since it depends on the political 'supply' offered to them.

The second consideration concerns the bourgeois bloc's ability to expand beyond its hard core. The other classes identified in our 2012 analysis differ from one another in terms of their expectations regarding economic policy, their positions on societal questions and immigration, and their self-positioning on the left–right axis.[32] Beyond the presence of an important popular-class element, another factor they have in common is that they share a strong desire for reduced unemployment and increased purchasing power. As it seeks to broaden its ranks, the bourgeois bloc thus faces several possibilities:

---

32   Amable, Guillaud and Palombarini, *L'Économie politique du néolibéralisme*.

it can, without questioning its foundational Europeanist and neoliberal commitments, open either to the 'left' by emphasizing its culturally progressive dimension, or to the 'right' by adopting harsher policies on immigration and welfare. But any attempt at a widening of the bourgeois bloc can succeed only on condition that the 'necessary' reforms supported by its hard core produce the fall in unemployment and the rise in purchasing power expected by the other elements of French society.

All in all, the most serious obstacle to the emergence of a bourgeois bloc in France is the structuring of the political 'supply'. The conditions for mediation between the groups likely to join the bloc's hard core do exist, and can easily be identified: they correspond to the pursuit of European integration and the structural reforms that go with it. While these groups are in the minority in social terms, they constitute a sufficiently solid political base for the bloc to become dominant, especially if neoliberal reforms produce the growth and the fall in unemployment a large part of the population so desires. What prevents the bourgeois bloc from emerging is the traditional structuring of the political 'supply' around the left–right divide. We can thus understand that, in the strategies of political leaders who seek the emergence of the bourgeois bloc, transcending political attachments in terms of 'right' and 'left' becomes a decisive task.

IS FRANCE FOLLOWING IN GERMANY'S FOOTSTEPS?

While the bourgeois bloc rallies together social groups who were once aggregated in each of the left- and right-wing blocs, it cannot itself be taken for a 'centrist' project. On numerous public policy questions, it is characterized by positions that are anything but 'moderate'. If the European question were to replace the left–right divide as the main axis of political differentiation, the strategy corresponding to the bourgeois bloc could itself be termed 'extreme'; in any case, it would leave no margins for mediation over the need to proceed with European integration within the treaties that have been signed, or indeed regarding the need for certain institutional reforms – especially those concerning various aspects of employment relations. The model of capitalism corresponding to the bourgeois bloc would result from a determined bid to push through a 'social-neoliberal' model. This would be based on structural changes to the labour market and the market for goods and services, which participation in the European project could both propel and provide with legitimacy.

It is thus not surprising that, after the PS and Hollande's election victory in 2012, France saw the resurgence of the 'German model' as an ideal to pursue, since it embodies the effort to overcome the contradictions inherent to the attempts to reform the labour market and social protection in a neoliberal direction. It does so as a continental European type of capitalism in which regulations in these fields are crucial to sociopolitical balances and economic performance. Governed by an SPD–Green coalition from 1998 to 2005, Germany deeply reformed the labour market and social protection even while preserving – for the moment at least – key elements of its economic competitiveness.[33] This made it possible in the early 2010s to parade its better performance in terms of unemployment, foreign trade and even growth than the rest of the Eurozone countries.[34] In 2013, President Hollande sang the praises of these reforms: 'As Gerhard Schröder has shown, progress is also about making courageous reforms in order to preserve employment [levels] and anticipate cultural and social shifts. We do not build anything solid if we ignore reality.'[35]

Germany had answered the apparently intractable problem of how to reconcile neoliberal reforms with the foundations of competitiveness in a non-neoliberal capitalist economy. It had done so by creating an outright dualism: aside from the core of workers whose skills were central to the model's competitiveness, there was a periphery whose employment and working conditions and access to the welfare state were weakened. This did not, for the moment at least, mean undermining the mechanisms for creating a skilled workforce, which are at

---

33 See Streeck, *Re-Forming Capitalism*.

34 At the cost of a clear increase in inequalities of status and income. In 2014, 8.8 per cent of people employed in France were low-wage workers – those earning under two-thirds of the median salary. The equivalent figure for Germany was 22.5 per cent. Eurostat press release 246, 8 December 2016.

35 Address by François Hollande upon the 150th anniversary of the German Social-Democratic Party, Leipzig, 23 May 2013.

the foundation of German industry's competitiveness. In more simple terms, the partial preservation of the continental European model for one segment of workers and application of the neoliberal model to another helped to lighten the burden – especially the fiscal one – that this second group represented on the first. For the moment, at least, this would stabilize the divide.

These transformations thus helped to constitute the equivalent of a bourgeois bloc that supported different coalitions, depending on the election concerned. These coalitions variously associated the Social-Democrats (SPD), conservatives (CDU/CSU), Liberals (FDP) and Greens, implementing policies that responded mainly to the demands of the core salariat and neglected most of the demands coming from workers in the secondary sector. The latter saw their expectations taken into consideration only by the radical-left Die Linke, subject to a long-term exclusion from government coalitions; thus far, the SPD has stubbornly rejected any prospect of a federal government coalition with the party, sometimes even extending this to the local level.

From 2012, France has thus followed the path that Germany already took in the early 2000s. This strategy, which invoked supposed 'realism' and the demands of competitiveness and the 'modernization' of the economy, marks a definitive break with the political and social unity of the left. All indications are that it is bringing about a profound restructuring of the French political landscape.

CHAPTER 4

The Processes of Political Recomposition

Political actors try to respond to social expectations in a selective manner, with a view to obtaining the support they need in order to achieve or retain power. In the political situation of France in the 2010s, the traditional structuring of the political 'supply' now appears as an obstacle to the satisfaction of sufficient numbers of mutually compatible expectations – and thus a barrier to the formation of a dominant bloc. On the right, the demand for a liberalization of the labour market and a sharp fall in taxes, as expressed by a section of business, private-sector managers and the self-employed (traders, artisans) entered into contradiction with the demands for protection coming from a large share of private-sector workers. On the left, European integration – and the neoliberal reforms it carried forth – divided social groups previously gathered within the same bloc.

The fracturing of the old social blocs is today a thirty-year-old process – and all the attempts to bring together a new dominant alliance within the current structures of the political system have met with failure. Increasing abstention, the rise of a party considered 'non-systemic' (the Front National), the result of the 2005 referendum, and the consistent electoral setbacks for incumbent governments are just so many consequences of a deep political crisis. The search for new mediation strategies – a quest the context of crisis has encouraged – ultimately produces two major systemic effects. On the one hand, the structuring of the political 'supply' has faced a mounting challenge from some political actors themselves. This is why some (sometimes opposed) strategies that are now taking root in France base themselves on a denunciation of a left–right divide, which they consider 'a matter of the past'. On the other hand, given how difficult it is either to renew old social alliances or to form new ones on the basis of the traditional factors of mediation, political actors have tended to attribute growing importance to new questions that can provide the material for hitherto unknown social pacts. This explains why questions of immigration, national identity or even secularism (*laïcité*) occupy at least as important a place in French political debate as fiscal policy, social protection or employment legislation.

Here we are, without doubt, still at the stage of exploring new paths for political mediation. Nothing guarantees that any one of these strategies will be a winner, forming a new dominant bloc and thus offering a way out of crisis. This is all the more true given that economic themes still appear decisive in defining the most widespread social expectations. But there is also no doubt that the political crisis is producing a restructuring of the French political 'supply'; and we should not overlook the effects that the centrality of themes like national identity and *laïcité* in dominant political (and media) discourse might have upon social demands. Indeed, we should not forget that political supply and demand are double-bound: in the short term, political action responds to existing expectations, but in the longer term it helps to orientate the way these expectations evolve. In particular, it helps to define the terrain of the 'possible' and of the 'reasonable' – constraints that individuals and social groups will gradually integrate into their expression of their expectations.

There are already two very visible dimensions of the restructuring of political supply, driven by political crisis: both the fragmentation of the left, first of all over the European question, and the new position taken up by the Front National.

THE LEFT'S FRAGMENTATION OVER THE EUROPEAN QUESTION

As we have emphasized, the divisions on the left regarding the pursuit and specific means of European integration – splits present ever since the first onset of European unity – burst into view during the 2005 referendum on the European Constitution. Since then they have continued to grow. These divisions affect not only political parties, but also the left's intellectuals of reference. If the left's intellectual and ideological output is unanimous in rejecting a neoliberal Europe, its proposals as to what route to follow are radically contradictory.

By way of example, let us look at the collective volume *Changer l'Europe!*, published by Les Économistes Atterrés.[1] This association brings together a large number of critical economists who 'powerfully want to see the economy liberated from neoliberalism', and whose activity consists of proposing 'alternatives to the austerity policies which today's governments call for'.[2] In the introduction to their collective volume, we can thus read that 'European integration must be resolutely inscribed within a strategy for the consolidation and development of the European social model. Europe must no longer set itself the objective of forcing its peoples to compete in a race to the bottom on social spending.' This is a shared objective, and an ambitious one; the authors are aware that 'policies can be transformed ... only if institutional-level ruptures are applied to the treaties themselves'. But what institutional ruptures are they talking about? As for the content of this treaty reform, or the future of the single currency, the authors' views part ways.

Thus, the book's final chapter, by Michel Dévoluy and Dany Lang, advocates a federal solution. This would mean carrying out a further transfer of sovereignty towards the European Union, while also respecting democratic process, and electing a genuinely European government by universal suffrage. The book's introduction makes clear that this position is far from shared among all the authors. Rather,

> many of them doubt that today the solution is to aim for a strengthened federalism, even if this means a 'democratic' federalism. They doubt this firstly because the current relations of force do not at all allow us to imagine such a turn. These '*Atterrés*' think, therefore, that at the present moment we should oppose any strengthening of federalism and endeavour, for a time at least, to restore powers and more freedom of manoeuvre to nation-states and peoples.[3]

---

1   Les Économistes Atterrés, *Changer l'Europe!* (Paris: Les Liens qui Libèrent, 2013).
2   See their website at atterres.org.
3   Les Économistes Atterrés, *Changer l'Europe!*, p. 20.

The transfer of sovereignty toward the Union and 'democratic' federalism; opposition to any strengthening of federalism and the return to national sovereignty: we would struggle to imagine viewpoints more distant from one another than these. The same goes for the future of the single currency. In the introduction to *Changer l'Europe!*[4] we can read that some of the authors consider that the malfunctioning of the euro and the imbalances that have built up 'demand that we contemplate a dissolution of the euro, or, at least, exit by some countries (or groups of countries)'. For this sub-group of Atterrés, keeping the euro in place is 'the surest means of destroying the European social model and driving Europe into decline'. Conversely, other Atterrés think that a reform of the way the Eurozone functions is the best solution, since the zone's 'break-up would mark a grave setback to European integration', which would translate into a loss of capacity to influence the evolution of the global economy and the promotion of the European social model.[5] We see, therefore, that, even while the objective is the same (defending the European social model), the strategies for achieving it – federalism and the single currency, versus national sovereignty and an exit from the euro – radically part ways.

In the constellation of critical economists, probably the sharpest (and most opposed) positions are those of Jacques Sapir and Alain Lipietz. For Sapir, 'political frameworks, institutions, are creations of history and they define national spaces as particular political spaces. It is in these particular political spaces that we have to find solutions'.[6] Sapir has no hesitation in proposing a new political front 'from the far left to neo-Gaullists' and even, on certain conditions, even the Front National. For him, European federalism is a necessarily anti-democratic product because the construction of legal frameworks that stand above nations – and thus outside the democratic control expressed within them – has always represented social and political regression. 'Today the European project advances at the same rate as the dismantling of democracy, not only in Europe but also within each

---

4   Its subtitle could be: 'Sure, but how?'

5   Les Économistes Atterrés, *Changer l'Europe!*, p. 21.

6   'Je suis démocrate donc souverainiste', interview with Jacques Sapir, *Horizons*, 12 October 2009.

of its member-states. The radical rejection of the federalist perspective goes hand-in-hand with French exit from the Eurozone: 'The interest to be had in euro exit is precisely that of conducting a really different policy, with the combination of industrial policies and incomes policy … but also capital controls and a financing of part of the public debt by the Central Bank.'

On the opposite end of things, Alain Lipietz judges that there is still a possible way out for Europe, precisely because

> Europe itself has sixty years' experience building a supranational space. At the end of the last century it failed to equip itself with a [form of] governance other than through rules – that is, a democratic and political [form of] governance – but there is nothing to stop the crisis itself forcing it to make a leap … A New Deal, but a Green New Deal. Europe has the material and institutional means to set itself such an objective, to save itself and contribute to saving the planet. But this demands a leap towards federalism. And therein lies what is doubtless the real obstacle: the lack of confidence in others, which reflects a lack of self-confidence.[7]

Between these two extremes we find a varied spectrum of viewpoints. One such example is the original stance taken by Frédéric Lordon. Hostile to the federalist project and looking favourably on euro exit, he nonetheless criticizes the 'champions of "national sovereignty"' for 'never [posing themselves] the question of who the incarnation of this sovereignty is.'[8] He differentiates a 'left sovereigntism [that] is easily distinguished from a right sovereigntism, the latter generally conceiving itself as the sovereignty "of the nation" whereas the former calls for respect for "popular" sovereignty'. This is not only a philosophical distinction: it has major implications for the profile of the social and political alliance that could unite around a rupture with the

---

7   Alain Lipietz, 'La trop évitable crise européenne', in Marie Auffray-Seguette, Jean-Marc Ferry and Arnauld Leclerc, eds, *Europe, Crise et Critique* (Paris: Presses de l'université Paris-Sorbonne, 2015).

8   The following citations are taken from Frédéric Lordon, *La Malfaçon. Monnaie européenne et souveraineté démocratique* (Paris: Les Liens qui Libèrent, 2014).

European project. For Lordon, right-wing sovereigntism is 'nothing other than the desire for a (legitimate) restoration of the means to govern, but exclusively handed to the particular governing forces in which "the nation" is invited to recognize itself – and hand itself over to. Left-wing sovereigntism is the other word for democracy – but understood in a slightly complicated sense.' Given that 'the imaginary of national sovereignty among the French right' is 'not yet unstuck from the figure of De Gaulle', it is hard to understand the mobilization stretching from the far left to some neo-Gaullists – and perhaps the Front National – that Sapir advocated.

Jacques Généreux's position is interesting, if only because this economist played an active political role in the French left as the Parti de Gauche's co-founder and national secretary for the economy between 2008 and 2013. For Généreux, it is necessary to complete the euro, filling in what the Eurozone would need to make it progressive. This is the idea that 'another Europe is possible', which has for years functioned as a unitary horizon for a deeply divided left. Généreux professes still to believe this, because France is 'one of the European Union's founder countries and ... Europe's secondmost economic power' – thus allowing France to mount a 'show of strength'.

For Généreux, a new (really left-wing) left government would propose an agreement to its European partners based on the conviction (it would have to be shared) that austerity policies can no longer be pursued. It would be necessary to implement different economic policies, in order to make it possible for France to remain in the Eurozone. But his heart is no longer in it. 'The problem is that this scenario will not come to pass. It is serious and credible, but there is no majority to carry it forward. While this does not happen, it is neoconservative, nationalist ... even neo-Nazi ... movements that scoop up the discontent in Europe and advocate a retreat [into the nation]'. Généreux acknowledges that, if 'the other Left' does exist in Europe, it is not progressing, precisely on account of its lack of clarity on the euro: 'Before the crisis we could say to voters: "We are Europeans, we want to refound Europe, create a test of strength" ... this could get a hearing. But no longer ... Europeans have suffered, some of them directly, the austerity policies that have been imposed ... So, today it is complicated to present yourself as pro-European: people laugh in your face.' What can be done in these conditions, to find a simple, audible discourse again? Généreux admits that this is where the whole difficulty lies. The threat of exit from the euro, addressed to the other European member-states, must be credible and fully embraced. But Généreux underlines the political difficulty of putting this tactic into practice:

> The Front de Gauche programme did not go that far, because the Parti Communiste was not prepared to go that far in disobeying the European rules. Yet this is the condition of the very credibility of this approach. We have to leave the ambiguity behind: the priority must be to implement a different policy. It is better to leave the euro in order to pursue a different policy than to abandon any other policy in order to save the euro. For ultimately it is Europe that we want to save, not the euro.[9]

Protecting the euro and making the leap towards a 'democratic' federalism; a European Green New Deal; a final attempt at negotiation with European partners before leaving the euro; a rupture and return to national sovereignty, while also taking a clear distance from 'right-sovereigntists'; or even a project for a new sovereigntist alliance running from the far left to neo-Gaullists: the least we can say is that the left has a lot of plans – and this would be no problem if they were compatible. But they are not. In reality, the only factor that would allow us today to use the left as an analytical category (here referring to a left that is actually left-wing) would be a rejection of neoliberal Europe: but 'on the left' there is no shared perspective on the European question. It has no common ideological and theoretical foundation; and, in such conditions, we understand the difficulties in offering anything on the 'supply' side of the political market. The slogan 'another Europe is possible' falls far short of hiding the left's fragmentation even on such fundamental questions as currency, institutional architecture, and relations with other European countries.

---

9 'La priorité, c'est de sauver l'Europe, pas l'euro', interview with Jacques Généreux, *Rue89*, 16 November 2013.

Added to these strategic difficulties are others of a directly political character. The Parti Communiste did not enter the governments
of either Jean-Marc Ayrault or Manuel Valls. But the Communists
remain the PS's allies in many regions, *départements* and *communes*. At
the national level, the Parti Communiste opposes the Parti Socialiste's
strategy of building the bourgeois bloc; it is, even so, rather complicated for voters to consider it a credible opponent to a party of which
it is consistently (and by obligation) the electoral ally. This situation
prompted Jean-Luc Mélenchon – in 2012 presidential candidate for the
Front de Gauche, which included the PCF – to ask 'how we became
so inscrutable'.[10] Mélenchon's reply was directly linked to the PCF's
electoral tactics: '[T]he example of the Grenoble municipal elections,
where part of the Front de Gauche chose to go in with the PS, is a
mirror that magnifies the national situation. The technique of the PCF
leaders – sometimes calling for alliance with the PS, sometimes appro-
priating the Front de Gauche – has watered down our message'.

Even so, these tactical doubts are only part of the problem – and
they clearly have less effect than the lack of any unitary strategy on
the European question – a problem decisive in outlining any political
supply able to get a hearing. We have emphasized that 'structural
reforms' (meaning: the neoliberal transformation of the French social
and economic model) conforming to the expectations among France's
European partners – especially Germany – are at the heart of the action
that seeks to construct a bourgeois bloc. Any opposition to such a
strategy requires that an alternative project be advanced. The intellectual and political fragmentation of the left over the European question
explains its impotence in occupying the social and electoral space of
opposition to the bourgeois bloc – a project which part of the (non-
Socialist) left may end up rallying to in the hope of influencing it and
softening the brutality of neoliberal reforms.

Like so many other things, politics abhors a vacuum. If the bourgeois bloc project does respond to *some* social expectations, it also
creates a vast space of opposition that the left has thus far been unable
to occupy. The possibility of representing the interests sacrificed by

---

10   Interview published in *Le Dauphiné libéré*, 21 August 2014.

the bourgeois bloc thus amounts to a political opportunity now being grasped by the Front National – even though a priori this party is very poorly placed to pose as an opponent of neoliberal reforms.

THE FRONT NATIONAL

Indeed, it was hardly predestined that the Front National would stand up as a defender of social protection and an opponent of neoliberal reforms and the European project. François Ruffin and the team at *Fakir* have reviewed 'forty years of Front National discourse' to highlight this party's U-turn.[11]

In keeping with its Poujadist origins, the Jean-Marie Le Pen of the early 1970s maintained a (paleo)liberal discourse 'heavily built on standing up for small traders and artisans'.[12] During the FN's early days the European question did occupy a big place in the party's propaganda materials, but not as one might expect if one hears the far-right party's current discourse on this question. 'The FN back then passionately championed European unity, with Jean-Marie Le Pen going as far as to envisage "giving up limited amounts of sovereignty" and, on the military terrain, "the coordination of French and British forces".[13] It is true, at the time the Soviet threat strongly conditioned far-right discourse on the need for the unity of the West. But Pierre Bousquet (who was the FN's treasurer) pushed the discourse on political integration very far. In the December 1972 issue of his review *Militant*, he championed the idea of a 'European federation provided with a federal executive, a federal parliament, a federal justice system, with each state maintaining its freedom to manage its domestic affairs and thus its own political system.[14] For much of its history the FN would remain pro-European. Thus, the FN's *Lettre parisienne* (spring 1988 issue) summarized one of Jean-Marie Le Pen's rallies in the following terms:

---

11 François Ruffin, *Pauvres Actionnaires. Quarante ans de discours économique du Front national passés au crible* (Amiens: Fakir Éditions, 2014).

12 Grégoire Kauffmann, 'Les origines du Front national', *Pouvoirs* 157: 2 (2016), p. 5.

13 Ibid., p. 12.

14 Ibid., pp. 12–13.

United by a robust anti-communist faith, beyond any language barriers, the young Europeans of 'Great Europe' received as their objective the fight for freedoms and in particular freedom for the peoples of Eastern Europe. In his speech, Jean-Marie Le Pen 'called for the construction of a political, economic and military Europe' and his intervention 'ended in a hearty mood to the notes of the *Ode to Joy* from Beethoven's Ninth Symphony and chants of "Europe, Le Pen, Freedom"'.

As Ruffin remarks, Maastricht was already by now within view; but the Front National nonetheless ended its rally with the EU's official anthem. Resolutely liberal in economic matters, the Front National of the 1980s saw Europe (as would others subsequently) as a possible accelerator to the 'necessary reforms'. Thus, in Le Pen's 1988 presidential campaign programme, we can read: 'Economy. Fewer taxes, less bureaucracy. For an adaptation of our economy to the European deadline for 1992, through a reduction in fiscal and social charges (especially employment taxes) which penalize French businesses compared to foreign competitors, and a review of income tax, which discourages economic activity and economic initiative. How? By putting the state on a diet'.

At the same time, the *frontistes* also placed their hopes in Europe to protect against the negatively judged effects of globalization. 'For a European Europe, protecting its borders from Third-World immigration and uncontrolled imports threatening its businesses', declaimed one FN leaflet in 1988. Liberal in their domestic economic programme, the FN have never been free-traders. But, according to the FN of the time, the protection against 'uncontrolled imports' from countries with low manpower costs should take place at the European borders.

The turn in its positions on Europe dates to the early 1990s. On the one hand, the collapse of the Soviet regime meant the European project was no longer justified as a rampart against 'Bolshevism'. On the other hand, the alignment of a large part of the left with pro-European positions left open the space to represent the interests sacrificed by Maastricht. A pure political animal, Jean-Marie Le Pen was not slow to take advantage of this. Thus, as early as 1992, he declared 'Maastricht Europe is a cosmopolitan and globalist Europe … Maastricht is even more taxes, the ruin of French agriculture, the dictatorship of the multinationals, the disappearance of the franc in favour of a single currency … We do not want a Europe of the bankers, so no to Maastricht.'[15] A supporter of European integration up until the late 1980s, in the following decade the Front National ensured itself a near-monopoly on the fight against 'Brussels's Europe'. Today, Marine Le Pen condemns 'Brussels's Europe [which] has everywhere imposed the destructive principles of ultra-liberalism and free trade, to the detriment of public services, jobs and fairness in society. To restore national sovereignty means, above all, to escape the suffocating and destructive Brussels straitjacket which we have been tied in against our own will.'[16] When she says this, she does so in continuity with this earlier volte-face.

The turn in the FN's evaluation of the effects of neoliberal policies in truth came much later. But it was perhaps even more abrupt than its volte-face over Europe. For many years, the FN's ultraliberal positions differentiated it from the right of Gaullist tradition. During the 1981 parliamentary election campaign Jean-Marie Le Pen declared: 'At first socialism is the welfare state, then it's the boss-state and then ends up as the kapo state. It is the multiplication of bureaucrats, of functionaries, of controls, of formalities, of tax, it is the ruin of businesses crushed under the weight of charges and taxes and threatened by the dictatorship of stratified banks and revolutionary trade unions.'[17] Ahead of the 1984 European elections, he insisted: 'To rebuild France, we must reduce the domain of the state, the number of civil servants, and public spending.' The models to follow were Ronald Reagan and Margaret Thatcher: as FN MP François Bachelot declaimed before the National Assembly,

We must rein in the state wherever we can. Yes, fewer civil servants! Fewer nationalized companies. Wherever there is less state, the French will always be the winners. I beg you: let's get rid of all

---

15 Cited in Ruffin, *Pauvres Actionnaires*.
16 Marine Le Pen, speech in Tours, 16 January 2011.
17 All the citations that follow are taken from Ruffin, *Pauvres Actionnaires*.

the regulations and allow the play of free competition. We have had enough of controls! That is our hope – a gulp of the liberal oxygen of free competition.

For the FN of the time, the interests that needed protecting were shareholder interests: 'How far will employee representation on company boards go?', the FN MP François Porteu de La Morandière asked the National Assembly on 29 April 1986:

> 7, 20, 50 per cent of board members? So, our demand is that you cancel this text in order to respect the rights of shareholders, the poor shareholders beaten up by years of socialism … It is your duty, and also in your interest, to respect shareholders' rights, because if not you will not win investors' confidence, and if you do not allow for investment there will be no jobs.

And we cannot say that social protection was at the heart of the *frontistes*' concerns. In 1986, Jean-Marie Le Pen called for France to imitate the United States, and in particular to review 'our social protection system, whose cost constantly climbs at a dizzying rate'.[18]

And this was how the FN's Bruno Mégret gave his backing to the Chirac government's privatization programme:

> We fully approve of the principles of a large-scale privatization like what you are offering us. This is the first beginning, since the war, of a retreat of the state and from socialism. The state should first of all devote itself to its own primary tasks, and the economy should become the prerogative of civil society again! But if the state does not have to produce televisions and monopolize ad spaces, we do not see why after 1991 it should continue to manufacture cars and produce railway lines.

He added:

---

18 *Journal officiel*, 23 April 1986.

To pull back the state, to trust economic actors again, to make citizens responsible – these are ambitions we fully sign up to. They are ours. We have always championed the liberalization of the economy as one of the preconditions for the renewal of our country. For too long France has been bogged down in the perversion of statism. The loss of competitiveness, the weakness of our industry, the deficiencies in its penetration of foreign markets, all our difficulties – including the cruellest, our 3 million unemployed – are irrefutable proof of the failure of interventionist, socialist or social-democratic recipes.

In the National Assembly, Jean-Marie Le Pen was categorical: 'Allow me to borrow a line from President Reagan, which did the rounds during his first election campaign: "I want the state to get off of my back and take its hand out of my pocket."' Thus, Le Pen quite simply demanded 'the abolition of income tax, phased out over five years' (23 April 1986), a business tax cut on the model of the one enacted by the conservative administration in the United States, and the immediate abolition of wealth tax ('Enough has been said already on the harmfulness of this tax, which has cost the economy and state a lot more than it has brought to the Treasury. But why wait for 1987 and not abolish it immediately?') Similarly, the FN boss criticized the Chirac government's tax amnesty, but because it was too harsh: 'A credible amnesty would have meant not demanding any penalty be paid, and it would have stipulated no reprisals for the four tax years preceding the date of repatriation' (15 June 1986).

The FN's positions on the state and fiscal questions would remain ultra-liberal throughout the 1990s. Thus, in 1995 the party promised that if it reached power, 'income taxes will be abolished within seven years' while 'the normal VAT rate will be increased by one point for a three-year period, with the sums thus collected fully devoted to reducing the state's debt'. Even later, in 2004, Marine Le Pen called for a 'massive reduction in the charges weighing down households and businesses' and proposed 'a great tax reform lightening the burden of taxes, rates and contributions which are suffocating our businesses, families and the French' – a reform that would once again set out 'the abolition of income tax'.

But then, just a few years later, this same Marine Le Pen proposed the 'rebuilding of the state' – this being 'the first condition of justice' – by giving it back 'the authority, the neutrality, a national consciousness and the means of functioning and of modernization which it needs'.[19] Within this approach, 'the priority will be to make income tax on physical persons more progressive, without making it heavier, by creating a new intermediate rate. The top rate of income tax will be taken to 46 per cent. Thus the middle classes will pay less income tax but very well-off households will pay more':

> The housing tax, which is opaque, will be integrated into income tax, [now] fairer, in the form of an added tax which will be as progressive as income tax. Taxes on dividends will be reviewed so that capital gains are not favoured over income on work. A single progressive tax on assets will be created, the fruit of the merger of property tax and wealth tax, on renewed bases that ensure tax justice.[20]

We thus see that Marine Le Pen's FN completely reversed the positions it had been pushing only a few years previously. It went from speaking of 'poor shareholders' to demanding a tougher tax regime for dividends; from the abolition of income tax to making it more progressive; from taking social security as a symbol of 'the habitual irresponsibility of the benefit-recipient citizen, and the state's taste for meddling everywhere without doing any good'[21] to defending social protection against neoliberal reforms; it went from calling the state 'the ruin of businesses' to insisting on the need to give it back 'means of operation' because this is the 'first condition of justice'.

Similarly, as late as 2006, Jean-Marie Le Pen criticized the demonstrations against the CPE labour law reform, commenting: 'I believe that the people who want to work will find employers, that the employers who want to hire will hire people worthy of being hired, and if they judge, in practice, that they are not capable of taking on the job they have been placed in, well, they're obliged to part ways.' Yet, only six

---

19   Marine Le Pen, speech in Tours, 16 January 2011.
20   Marine Le Pen, *Mon projet*, 2012 presidential election.
21   *National Hebdo*, 16 November 1995.

years later, his daughter reckoned that '[t]he proliferation of unchosen part-time work and the untamed spread of short-term contracts throw a section of the workforce into precarious financial straits ... Shock precarity did not have to happen!'[22]

As François Ruffin writes, it is rather dizzying to hear Marine Le Pen rail against 'the dogmas of ultra-liberalism', the 'untrammelled reign of King Money', the 'super-rich who sell our work, our heritage', to hear her mock a 'president who ought not to be the governor of an American protectorate' or vaunt 'the state's role in regulating economic matters', when the Front National was itself the most dogged in trashing 'the state's regulatory role', the most zealous in singing the praise of the 'American model', the most fanatical in lauding these 'dogmas of ultra-liberalism'.[23]

Marine Le Pen's 'new FN' thus partly built itself around a radical and more or less sincere shift on the themes most present at the time of Jean-Marie Le Pen's leadership. As Cécile Alduy remarks, the FN's contemporary discourse has dropped markers of far-right vocabulary like anti-Semitism and explicit biological racism; but this lexical shift has been accompanied 'by a shrewd mixture of triangulation toward the Left on economic and republican questions and securing voter loyalty over questions of culture and identity'.[24]

But even if it is addressed towards the worst-off classes of wage-earners, has this discourse actually worked? Based on the results of L'enquête électorale française: comprendre 2017, a survey carried out for Cevipof by Ipsos from 20 to 29 November 2015, the voting intentions for FN candidates at the first round of the 2015 regional elections were as follows: 46 per cent among blue-collar workers, 41 per cent among white-collar employees, 35 per cent among self-employed professions and 33 per cent among farmers. These figures seem to indicate that the FN has partly achieved its objective. But counterbalancing this is the reality of high levels of abstention. Another telling consideration is the fact that the FN's vote was strong among private-sector employees (35 per cent) but also – and this is also a new phenomenon – among their

---

22 Marine Le Pen, press release, 17 December 2012.
23 Ruffin, Pauvres Actionnaires.
24 Cécile Alduy, 'Nouveau discours, nouveaux succès', Pouvoirs 157: 2 (2016), p. 25.

public-sector counterparts (30 per cent). We may also note that the FN remains comparatively weak among the best-off categories: only 18 per cent of top managers vote FN, along with 15 per cent of people with an educational level of *baccalauréat* + 4 (or higher) and 19 per cent of those in a household with a monthly income above €6,000.

There is thus a 'popular-class' basis for the FN's electoral support. But it is not clear that this should be related to the party's volte-face on economic questions.[25] Indeed, this is a more or less hesitant turn, as we see if we look more attentively at Marine Le Pen's relatively ambiguous statements on this or that question, in particular Frexit. Asked by a journalist whether this would be a possibility if the FN won the 2017 election, the party's leader replied: 'There has never been any question of that.'[26] Similarly, the idea periodically re-emerges of 'reorientating' the FN's economic proposals towards small and micro-enterprises, with a view to eating up more of the richer parts of the electorate.

An analysis of polls for the 2012 election[27] clearly shows the close association between electoral support for the FN and support for a more traditional liberal right. The reasons for *frontiste* sympathies in fact align with the motives for supporting traditional right-wing parties (and, of course, stand opposed to those that turn voters towards left-wing parties): a harsh view of unemployed people's efforts to seek work, hostility towards immigrants, a lack of support for government efforts to reduce inequalities, and so on. In this sense, the political bases of support for the FN in fact look very similar to those for parties of the so-called 'republican' right.

Without doubt, the FN's discourse is different from what it was in the 1980s. But the party's electoral base seems to have expanded without transforming. Contrary to what the rhetoric of some of its leaders would have us believe, hopes of a 'Thatcherite' rupture are still widespread among its supporters.

---

25 Empirical analysis of 2012 electoral surveys in Bruno Amable, *Structural Crisis and Institutional Change in Modern Capitalism: French Capitalism in Transition* (Oxford, Oxford University Press, 2017) shows that FN support mainly rested on classically right-wing expectations in the field of economic policy. This would cast in much more relative terms the impact that the tactical turn made by Marine Le Pen and her advisers has had on the FN's electoral success.

26 Interview for TF1.

27 See Amable, *Structural Crisis and Institutional Change.*

EIGHT POLITICAL PROJECTS FOR A NEW POLITICAL SPACE

The political crisis that has followed the fracturing of the old social alliances has given new impulse to the old project of building a bourgeois bloc. The growing strength of this project has introduced a new cleavage in the spectrum of political 'supply' in France.[28] On the one hand are the supporters of the European Union and the reforms it demands; on the other, those who want a return to national sovereignty and an exit from the euro.

Nonetheless, the traditional opposition between political left and right remains. This is not only because it still very largely structures political 'supply' in France, but also because the new cleavage is very far from able to represent the full spectrum of society's reactions to neoliberal reforms.[29] It is clear that the 'Europeanist' pole occupied by the bourgeois bloc favours transition to the neoliberal model; yet the 'sovereigntist' side has no settled position on this question, and we could even say that the position that favours the neoliberal transformation of French capitalism is dominant therein. The Front National's history is rooted in ultra-liberalism; its recent *transformismo* should not lead us to forget the fact that the large majority of its leading personnel do still favour neoliberal reforms. Similarly, the economic programme of Nicolas Dupont-Aignan, 'sovereigntist' candidate in the 2017 presidential contest, was very clearly liberal in inspiration.[30] Under the heading, 'Free up the living forces of French industry' we find, for instance, the assertion of the need 'to reform the state to limit wastage and the squandering of public money', the need to 'stop building up the debt burden for future generations' and even the idea of 'cutting back the forest of regulation and legislation and reducing social charges' and 'ensuring total equivalence between private- and public-sector employees'. If political 'supply' entirely restructured itself around the Europeanist/sovereigntist cleavage, the many social interests sacrificed by neoliberal reforms would thus find themselves largely

---

28   Here we use the term 'cleavage' in the narrower political-science sense, rather than the dictionary definition.

29   According to a recent survey, 48 per cent of French people consider themselves 'left-wing', as against 52 per cent 'on the right'. Ifop, 'Être de gauche aujourd'hui', September 2016.

30   Available at debout-la-france.fr.

underrepresented. This suggests that the left–right divide inherited from the past is not disappearing any time soon.

We can attempt to project French political 'supply' across two axes (without wishing to claim that the dimensions of the political space can be reduced to just two). Indeed, following the works of political scientists like Herbert Kitschelt, it has regrettably become all too common to represent the political space as necessarily having two dimensions.[31] In this schema, the first axis corresponds to the traditional left–right cleavage on economic policy questions; the second sets out an opposition of a cultural or 'societal' nature equivalent to differences between 'authoritarian' or 'liberal' conceptions of so-called 'social mores'. Our approach in this section does not follow this same logic. Rather, it seeks to map out the possible decompositions and recompositions within an evolving political space on the basis of two cleavages we consider essential to explaining the current transformations in political 'supply'. Moreover, while the cleavages that we have identified do have a 'cultural' (or ideological) dimension, both have to do with economic and institutional politics.

The two axes differentiating political supply, as represented in Figure 4.1, first of all allow us to identify four homogenous groups. The position of the pro-EU neoliberals (A) is that occupied by Les Républicains. It corresponds to the programmes for the 2017 primaries issued by Alain Juppé, François Fillon and Bruno Le Maire.[32]

The pro-European Left quadrant (B) corresponds to the traditional positioning of the Parti Socialiste and its satellites. However, as we have already seen, the difficulty of meaningfully reconciling left-wing policies and respect for the European treaties, as well as the fracture this difficulty creates within the left-wing bloc, has pushed the Parti Socialiste to reorientate its strategy towards the construction of a

---

31 The Terra Nova document on 'La France de demain' is one of the most sinister examples of how this portrayal is used.

32 By way of example, in his programme Bruno Le Maire proposed the classic neoliberal–right-wing list: reasserting state authority, lower public spending, kick-starting competitiveness by cutting business taxes, 'modernizing' the labour market (by attacking French employment law as a barrier to hiring), and so on. At the same time, Le Maire insisted on his attachment in the EU, which France should 'relaunch' by playing the role of an 'engine' therein.

Figure 4.1 The new space of political offerings

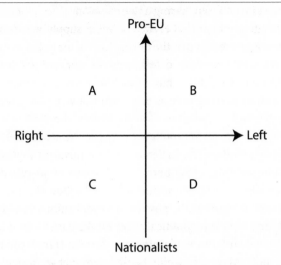

bourgeois bloc, which implies a repositioning of the PS within the overall political space.

Dupont-Aignan's programme corresponds to a sovereigntist and liberal pole (C): this was also the Front National's position under Jean-Marie Le Pen's leadership.

Jean-Luc Mélenchon has instead tended to occupy the 'sovereigntist' left space (D), even more markedly since the break in his alliance with the Parti Communiste.[33]

The fragmentation of political 'supply' linked to the opposition between Europeanists and sovereigntists – an opposition that cuts across the traditional battle between left and right – has also had a more particular consequence. It means that each of these four projects represents only a minority of French society. The formation of a new dominant social bloc and a way out of political crisis presuppose the establishment of an alliance able to transcend one of the two cleavages.

---

33 For convenience, we have adopted these commonplace terms of political debate, though a lot more could be said about them, especially the notion of 'sovereignty'. We have already referred to the different definitions of this term given by Sapir and Lordon.

We might characterize the cases identified in Figure 4.1 as four 'identitarian' projects. But added to these there are four other projects, founded on compromises that unite their supporters along one of these axes while side-lining the other.

The first alliance project is the bourgeois bloc (A + B). It is based on the 'transcendence' (or, rather, the elimination) of the left–right cleavage, instead making support for the European Union the dominant dimension of its political offer. As we have stressed in previous chapters, this project is the product of a long ideological development. It is coherent both from the viewpoint of its fundamental public policies (the supposedly 'necessary reforms' of neoliberal stamp) and that of its social base, as it gathers the middle- and upper-ranking categories previously assembled in both the left- and right-wing bloc. The bourgeois bloc is in the minority, in social terms; but, in its bid for success, it can count on the dispersion and abstention of the popular classes.[34] On François Hollande's initiative, the most widely shared perspective within the Parti Socialiste was precisely the formation of such a bloc. However, the persistence of the left–right divide – and the resulting electoral gains to be had from the call to cast a 'useful vote' – have stopped the Parti Socialiste from openly parading this strategy.

Paradoxically, it was thus a candidate from outside PS ranks – but who was for a long time economy minister in the Socialist government – who most clearly articulated the rupturing of the old alliances and the need to establish new ones. This was Emmanuel Macron. As he told France Inter on 4 September 2016, in 1983–84 there was a 'schism within the left'; 'there is today a realistic left which wants things to change … and there is a conservative, status-based left … I am from this realistic left, my political line of descent is Mendès France, it's Michel Rocard'. For Macron, the two lefts are irreconcilable. The 'only possibility' is an alliance between the 'realistic left' and part of the right:

> In this realistic left there is a will … to regain the strength of the national story, to build it through a more ambitious European policy … through deep reforms in [this] country. This realistic left has to

---

34 See Bruno Amable, Elvire Guillaud and Stefano Palombarini, *L'Économie politique du néolibéralisme. Le cas de la France et de l'Italie* (Paris: éd. Rue d'Ulm, 2012).

speak with centrists, it has to speak with the right that shares these values, because there is a right which we could call Orléanist and French liberal, which is much closer to this realistic left than it is to Nicolas Sarkozy or right-wing conservatives.

The PS prime minister Manuel Valls had previously made similar statements[35] but changed his attitude in the run-up to the 2017 election.[36]

Symmetrically opposed to the construction of a bourgeois bloc is the building of a sovereigntist bloc (C + D). This, in turn, supposes the at least temporary transcending of the left–right divide in the interest of leaving the euro, and (possibly) the European Union itself. The economist Jacques Sapir has made no bones about his efforts to promote a 'Front' of this type: 'Once we set dismantling the Eurozone as a priority objective, a broad-union strategy, including right-wing forces, seems not only logical but also necessary', he writes.[37] And he makes clear: 'Ultimately the question of relations with the Front National, or with the party that emerges from [it] will be posed. It should be understood that it's clearly no longer time for sectarianism or for either side denying the other the right to be there.'[38]

But what future would a sovereigntist alliance have? What would happen to it once it achieved its objective of Frexit? According to Sapir, the government that resulted from the Sovereigntist Front would have to enact a programme

not only to dismantle the euro but also to organize the economy 'the day after'. This programme implies a particular effort in terms of investment, but also a new currency regime, as well as new rules for state action in the economy. Moreover, it would imply a new conception of the European Union's future form and, in the case of France in particular, a general reform of the tax system. So we slip, almost

---

35   Referring to the 'irreconcilable' lefts, for instance in a speech in Corbeil in February 2016.

36   In October 2016, Valls called for the left to unite ahead of the presidential election.

37   Jacques Sapir, 'Les perspectives d'un Front contre l'euro', at russeurope.hypotheses. org, 1 August 2015.

38   Sapir, 'Réflexions sur la Grèce et l'Europe', at russeurope.hypotheses.org, 21 August 2015.

without noticing, from the logic of exiting, or dismantling, the euro towards a logic of reorganizing the economy.[39]

This project's coherence depends precisely on these policies for 'the day after' – and they are particularly ambitious. For Sapir, exit from the euro resembles opening a door: '[I]t's pointless to be fussy about who it is that opens it.' Without fear of contradiction, he writes that once 'the door is open, the question of the direction we will then take will be posed, and that is where the differences between "Left" and "Right" will recover their full meaning'.[40] Hence, while the (temporary) overcoming of the left–right divide serves his political project, Sapir is well aware that the differences among the sovereigntists, especially on economic policy matters, are profound.

The problem is that – as we have just seen – Sapir's project is not limited to leaving the euro. If exit is to produce the hoped-for results, it has to be followed by the ambitious policies for 'the day after'. But how could the differences between left and right not affect the redefinition of the role of the state, public investment programmes, new monetary rules, relations with EU countries, tax reforms – in short, the very 'reorganization of the economy' Sapir considers necessary to any successful handling of the return of monetary sovereignty? It is not hard to foresee how, faced with these problems, the Sovereigntist Front would explode as soon as Frexit was realized, before the implementation of the political programme articulated by Sapir. Confronted with their programmatic differences and the contradictions they create, the architects of the Sovereigntist Front (in whose ranks we must count, alongside Sapir, the liberal Nicolas Dupont-Aignan and former Front National member Florian Philippot) have tended gradually to sideline economic questions and place emphasis not only on sovereignty but also on secularism (laïcité) and national identity – ideas on which they can much more easily reach agreement.[41]

---

39   Ibid.

40   'Theresa May et le changement de paradigme', blogpost by J. Sapir, at russeurope. hypotheses.org, 9 August 2016.

41   Between June and September 2016, Sapir devoted twenty-four blogposts to sovereignty, laïcité and French identity, including five on the Nice attack and three on the 'burkini' controversy.

These considerations apply to a front between many parties, which – particularly given Jean-Luc Mélenchon's refusal to participate – will never see the light of day. But they also apply to the Front National's new positioning. At Marine Le Pen's initiative, the FN has tried to free itself of the far-right label and to build a sovereigntist front of its own. 'We are neither right nor left'[42] has thus, after many years, (again) become the slogan of a party whose economic programme combines the ultra-liberal tradition with a new Keynesian interventionism, and builds its unity on the themes of French identity, national sovereignty and rejection of immigration. This means that the expectations of its social base are largely contradictory: the demands for the defence of social protection coexist with others calling for its dismantling. The party would struggle to maintain its unity through a spell in government.

The third 'compromise' project corresponds to a reunification of the left-wing bloc (B + D). As we have indicated, the European question – and in particular all that it entails in terms of structural transformations and economic policy – puts up obstacles to the viability of such a project. The slogan 'Another Europe is possible' is utterly exhausted, and no longer has any political effectiveness. Only the leadership of the Parti Communiste still seems attached to it, more for electoralist reasons (in order to renew its alliance with the PS) than out of strategic conviction.[43] However, the reconstruction of a social alliance on the left is probably Jean-Luc Mélenchon's future horizon. The France Insoumise candidate initially occupied the space of the sovereigntist left: 'the nation', he argued in an interview for l'Humanité,

is a word that belongs to the progressive camp. It has been recuperated by the right. I thus call for serious reflection, not based on impulse. In France it is the Republic that founds the nation and not the other way around. The nation makes up part of the revolutionary strategy

---

42   Marine Le Pen, rally at Paris's Zénith, April 2012. The 'neither left or right' posture has a long history on the far-right.

43   For instance, 'Brexit. Pierre Laurent: "L'ampleur du désaveu doit conduire à la refondation de l'UE"', L'Humanité, 24 June 2016.

that I defend, as the framework in which democracy is exercised and as a cornerstone of the popular will.[44]

In accordance with this stance, he repudiated any prospect of an alliance with the Parti Socialiste, but also – at least during the election campaign – with the Parti Communiste. According to Mélenchon, 'Rallying "the left" together would prevent the people's own federation'.[45] The sharpness of his position drew virulent attacks against Mélenchon,[46] but also allowed him to climb rapidly in the polls.

We will add that – conscious of the depth of the fractures that divided the old social alliance on the left – Mélenchon tried to shake off his label as the 'left-wing' candidate: he said that he was addressing 'the people' in the name of the 'general human interest'. But the very clear refusal to participate in a sovereigntist front with right-wing and – even more so – far-right candidates, as well as the preference to renegotiate the European treaties before exiting, allow us to imagine that a two-phase strategy was at work here.[47] First, his task was to build a new hegemony over the left – possible if he beat the Socialist candidate in the first round of the presidential election; then it was to rally a social alliance of the left on a new basis, supposing either a major rewriting of the European treaties or exit from the euro. The horizon for such a strategy clearly extended beyond the 2017 electoral campaign, for which reason the chances of victory for a candidate backed by the traditional left-wing bloc seemed close to nil.

There remains one last 'compromise' project, which, in the aftermath of the 2017 election, no one was proposing openly: the

---

44 'Le rassemblement de la "gauche" empêcherait le peuple de se fédérer', interview for *L'Humanité*, 20 September 2016.

45 Ibid.

46 For example, by Olivier Besancenot, for whom 'Jean-Luc Mélenchon makes big statements on economic sovereigntism … But ultimately you muddy the waters on freedom of movement. And then you no longer stutter and you come to say that you aren't for freedom of movement. I see all that as major political regression, for the radical left' – hors-serie.net, 27 September 2016.

47 Mélenchon tweeted on 22 September 2016: 'The Front national is the banalization of evil.' For instance, in an interview published in *Le Monde* on 25 June 2016, Mélenchon declared: 'My first task will be to renegotiate the treaties, and if that doesn't work, we move on to plan B'.

reunification of the right-wing bloc (A + C). That no candidate spoke to such a programme was the result of two factors. One was the Front National's strategy – as it endeavoured to position itself on the sovereigntist pole while transcending the left–right divide; the other was the heritage of the 'front républicain' and all that it implied – namely, the so-called 'governmental' parties closing ranks against the Front National. Yet it was far from certain that these factors would remain operative for very long. There were very major contradictions in the Front National's economic programme, and its pre-2017 election shift was only a façade driven by its electorally orientated *transformismo*.

As for the 'front républican', it seemed only to be upheld by the Parti Socialiste, whereas for a significant part of the right it was nothing more than a distant memory.[48] The fracturing of the right-wing bloc is linked to contradictory expectations within the social groups of which it is composed, with regard to policies such as the strong liberalization of the labour market, lower taxes and benefit payments, and a reduction of social protections. This fracture runs through the electoral base of the Front National as well as that of the Républicains – indeed, it seems that we can hardly rule out an ultimate recomposition of the political supply on the right. If the left's split over the European question seems a deep one, difficult to repair, the rupture on the right could be overcome by an evolution of these two parties. That is, they could meet each other on the ground of ultra-liberal and Eurosceptic (in a word, Thatcherite) positions, while abandoning the Europeanist part of the republican right to the bourgeois bloc and leaving the waged fraction of the Front's popular-class electorate either without representation or, perhaps, as part of a renewed left-wing bloc.

A development of this type – of which the triumphal selection of François Fillon in the 2017 Republicans' primaries offered something of an anticipation – would be even likelier if the Front National won the next presidential election and mounted a more or less sincere

---

48 Already in the 2011 local elections, Sarkozy declared that the UMP's approach to the run-off votes was 'neither PS or FN'. Asked what their position would be if the 2012 presidential election produced a run-off between the PS and the FN, Sarkozy and Jean-François Copé both said they would not give any indication of how to vote. In the 2015 regional elections, the UMP decreed that there should be no 'stepping aside or merging with Socialist lists' in the case of 'three-cornered' contests – i.e. those setting the PS and UMP against the FN.

attempt to take France out of the euro. The formation of a social bloc under the banner of an authoritarian and conservative (neo)liberalism, driven by a rapprochement between the Front National and the 'republican' right, seems like a probable scenario, given the current balance of forces and configuration of social expectations being expressed.

CHAPTER 5

France's Model of Capitalism, at the Heart of Political Conflict

Whoever can recognise his own forces and those of his enemy is rarely vanquished.

Machiavelli

An analysis of France's structural crisis must be based on a consideration of four connected factors. These factors are: 1) the institutions that define a particular model of capitalism; 2) social alliances, and in particular the dominant social bloc formed by groups who back the ruling parties' policies – and thus the particular model of capitalism to which these policies contribute; 3) the political structure, and in particular the dominant political actors and the strategy they deploy in order to aggregate, stabilize or modify the dominant social bloc; and 4) the policy pursued, especially in the economic domain, to respond to the short-to-medium-term expectations of the dominant social bloc.

The rise of Emmanuel Macron stands in continuity with a political endeavour that has itself shaped these four elements. Indeed, ever since the 1970s – with Valéry Giscard d'Estaing's presidency and Raymond Barre's actions as prime minister – the transformation of French capitalism has taken place under the sign of 'neoliberalization'. In short, this means the dismantling of the socioeconomic model that prevailed during the 'Trente Glorieuses'.

This shift has affected most social institutions, but the transformation has not taken place in a linear or continuous way. Some domains have been profoundly changed, while others, more important to the stability of the dominant bloc, have been only marginally affected, at least until Hollande's presidency. As we have seen, this transformation has led to the rupturing of the traditional social blocs, on the right and especially on the left. This rupture is owed to the growing gap between the expectations of certain groups within each bloc and, on the other hand, the policies that parties of left and right have actually enacted.

This has led each of them to the search for an alternative social bloc. The right did so impressionistically, when Giscard d'Estaing sketched out a social project for 'two-thirds of France'. But the left has done so increasingly forcefully, to the point that this effort became practically explicit during Hollande's spell in office. The Parti Socialiste's search for an alternative social bloc proceeded by way of a redefinition of its political alliances – the explicit objective of some in the party, at least since Jacques Delors's hope of achieving the union of 'wise men from all sides'.[1] The economic policy the PS has followed since the late 1970s, with the exception of the early months of 1981, has been subordinated to deflation, the nominal anchoring of the franc to the deutschmark, and then monetary union, culminating in the euro. This has itself contributed to the rupturing of the two traditional social blocs, complementing developments in the rest of the four factors mentioned above.

Emmanuel Macron's bid for the presidency appeared to represent a break with the traditional political game. Indeed, there were certain factors that pointed to its novelty: Macron had never previously held any elected position, but won the presidency in 2017 at less than forty years of age. His political movement En Marche !, which later became La République En Marche ! (LREM) was founded barely a year before the presidential election; yet, in summer 2017, it won a majority in the National Assembly, sending a large number of first-time MPs with no political experience to the Palais Bourbon. Certainly, part of Macron's success should be attributed to this impression of renewal, which he was able to spread among the electorate and the media. But we do not have to look very closely into Macron's trajectory to set it directly in continuity with the transformation of the French model we have already described. Author of the *Rapport Attali* during Sarkozy's presidency, during Hollande's spell in office Macron was general secretary adjunct to the president's office, and then economy minister. He effectively inspired, conceived and supervised the economic policy and

---

1   Philippe Alexandre and Jacques Delors, *En sortir ou pas* (Paris: Grasset, 1985).

the 'structural reforms' enacted during Hollande's presidency, from CICE to the Loi Travail via the bill bearing his own name (the Bill for Growth, [Economic] Activity and Equal Opportunities, known as the Loi Macron).

The new president's actions in office since 2017 have continued the reorientation of political alliances that commenced under Hollande – indeed, they have practically brought it to its conclusion. Hollande sought the support of the bourgeois bloc, but did so after he had been elected by the left-wing bloc. Conversely, ever since Macron first began his bid for the presidency, he has deliberately chosen to turn his back on the two traditional blocs. The Hollande-era Parti Socialiste tried to reconcile the (even partial) support it received from the left-wing bloc with the emergence of a new social bloc. Macron, instead, ignored the PS, a party that had now been marginalised. Indeed, his LREM can do without political alliances, and can thus claim to represent the bourgeois bloc alone. It is not looking for political alliances with the traditional left- or right-wing formations, but rather to destroy them, and to rally a significant part of these blocs behind LREM itself. The bourgeois bloc is simultaneously both cohered and represented by Macron and LREM; it supports the policy of radical neoliberal 'reforms' and the 'pro-capital' economic policy his government pursues.

Faced with the new government's orientation – and the action it is pursuing with both speed and determination – opposition parties and movements still seem to lack any clearly defined strategic course. They essentially base themselves on what remains of the old left- and right-wing blocs – a heterogeneous set of social groups mutually opposed on numerous essential subjects, starting with economic policy.

MACRON'S VICTORY: THE BOURGEOIS BLOC'S TRIUMPH

Emmanuel Macron was elected president in spring 2017, to the (feigned) surprise of the great majority of analysts and commentators. His victory was partly the consequence of Les Républicains' uninspired decision to run François Fillon as their candidate. But, more significantly, it was the outcome of the social and political dynamic we have analysed in this book – a long-term dynamic that began back in the

1980s. On the one hand, the crisis of the social alliances of right and left – which, as we have shown, is linked to old and deep contradictions – has come out into the open with the elimination of both Les Républicains' candidate and the PS contender Benoît Hamon in the first round. Moreover, the one-quarter of voters (24 per cent) who lifted Macron to first place in the first round corresponds to a social coalition very similar to the bourgeois bloc.

<h2 style="text-align:center">A NEW SOCIAL BASE</h2>

The disintegration of the old alliances tells us why the new government's base really is 'above left and right'. In the first round of the presidential election, Macron received the votes of half of those who had picked François Hollande (48 per cent) and François Bayrou (52 per cent) back in 2012, but also 17 per cent of those who had voted for Sarkozy, and even 10 per cent of those who had voted for Jean-Luc Mélenchon.[2] Contrary to what a widespread and strongly felt intuition might suggest, the decomposition of a political landscape based on the opposition between right and left has not weakened the link between class belonging and electoral behaviour. Rather, it has done the exact opposite. The social alliances of right and left corresponded to pacts between a fraction of the bourgeois classes and a fraction of the popular classes. This is not the case with the bourgeois bloc, whose principle is precisely the unity of the middle and upper classes, combined with the general exclusion of the popular classes.

Thus, at the first round of the 2017 presidential election, Macron polled strongest among managers and upper professionals (37 per cent) and weakest among blue-collar workers (15 per cent); he hit 35 per cent among voters with a second or third university degree, but only 17 per cent of those without a *baccalauréat* (school-leaving certificate) – a category among whom he ranked fourth behind Le Pen

---

2   Unless otherwise indicated, the survey data cited here are drawn, for the presidential election, from Ifop, *Le profil des électeurs et les clefs du premier tour de l'élection présidentielle* (April 2017); and, for the legislative election, from Ifop, *Le profil des électeurs et les clefs du premier tour des élections législatives* (June 2017). These are cited below as Ifop (2017P) and Ifop (2017L), respectively.

(31 per cent), Mélenchon (20 per cent) and even Fillon (18 per cent). The accentuation of class divides during the last presidential election is also underlined, indeed forcefully so, by the relationship between voting patterns and income levels. In the first round, Macron's score among voters with household incomes below €1,250 a month was 14 per cent; it rose to 18 per cent among the category between €1,250 and €2,000, 25 per cent for those between €2,000 and €3,000, and 32 per cent for those earning over €3,000. If we factor in abstention rates (which are higher among popular-class categories) the class profile of the new social alliance comes out even more strongly: Macron won the support of 10 per cent of those on household incomes under €1,250 a month, whereas he was chosen by 27 per cent of potential voters whose income was over €3,000 a month.[3]

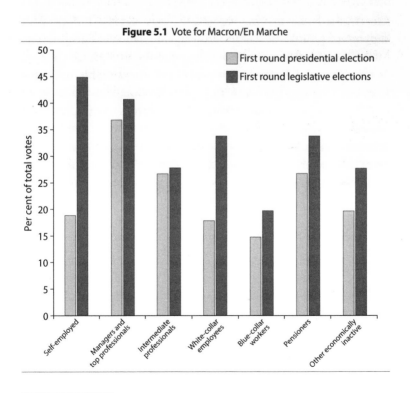

Figure 5.1 Vote for Macron/En Marche

---

3   Ipsos, *1er tour. Sociologie des électorats et profil des abstentionnistes*, April 2017.

The electorate that picked LREM candidates at the first round of the legislative (parliamentary) elections was similar to this, not least as LREM picked up a significant fraction of the voters who had backed Fillon in the presidential contest. According to surveys, between 21 and 30 per cent of those who had supported the right-wing candidate in that contest chose to support the new presidential majority in the first round of the legislative elections.[4] LREM's success particularly corresponded to the fact that the self-employed turned towards the party in massive numbers; in April, only 19 per cent had picked Macron, but, two months later, 45 per cent voted for an LREM candidate.[5]

AN ELECTORATE UNITED BY SUPPORT FOR THE EU, DIVIDED OVER NEOLIBERAL REFORMS

Clearly, the factor that has allowed this new alliance to form is its supporters' positive view of the growing integration of European and international markets. In the first round of the presidential election, Macron obtained the support of 39 per cent of voters who considered themselves among the 'winners of globalization', whereas he stood at only 12 per cent among those who perceived themselves as its 'losers' (and 31 per cent of those who said they were 'neither winners or losers').[6] Almost three in five of the new president's voters (57 per cent) believed that France should 'open up more to the world'. Similarly, Macron was the only candidate whose electorate mostly (58 per cent) thought that, 'faced with competition from low-wage countries', France should 'accept the game of global competition and rely on the quality and reliability of its products.' A majority of each of the other candidates' electorates chose the alternative response – namely that France should 'protect itself by setting up trade barriers at the borders.'[7]

---

4   Ifop (2017L); Nicolas Sauger, *French Electoral Study 2017* (Paris: Centre d'Etudes Européennes, Sciences Po, 2018). We will cite this text as FES 2017.

5   Ifop (2017L).

6   Ifop (2017P).

7   This was the response chosen by 53 per cent of Fillon's voters, 55 per cent of Hamon's, 57 per cent of Mélenchon's and 79 per cent of Le Pen's. Ifop, *Ce que veulent les Français – Volet 2* (December 2017).

Figure 5.2 Optimism regarding France's future (by political self-positioning)

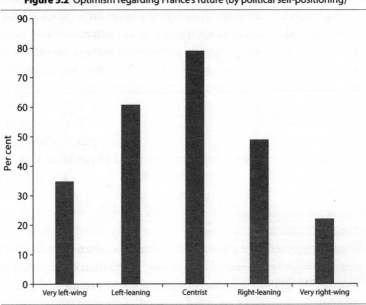

In keeping with a position largely sympathetic to an opening to competition and free trade, the new government's social base almost unanimously supported France's EU membership. This support was a majority sentiment across the whole French population (66 per cent of those surveyed considered France's EU membership 'mostly a good thing'), which was also the case among all socio-occupational categories, with levels varying from timid support among blue-collar workers (56 per cent) and the self-employed (56 per cent) to the enthusiastic backing of managers and upper categories (80 per cent). But among Macron's electorate, the level of support for France's place in the EU was even higher than among managers, reaching 88 per cent.[8]

Unsurprisingly, the voters who chose Macron in the first round of the presidential contest were near-unanimously optimistic about France's future (87 per cent) as well as their own and their families' future (80 per cent). At the other end of this optimism scale was Marine Le Pen's electorate, at 29 and 35 per cent respectively. This question on

8   Ifop, *Ce que veulent les Français.*

attitudes regarding the future sheds further light on the new profile of class conflict produced by the disintegration of the old political divides. On the one hand, optimism has almost no correlation with the left–right axis; but there is a very clear – and hardly surprising – correlation between optimism and income.[9]

OPTIMISM REGARDING FRANCE'S FUTURE (ACCORDING
TO MONTHLY HOUSEHOLD INCOME)

What allowed Macron to come out on top in the first round of the presidential election was his capacity to present himself as the candidate who best guaranteed France's continuing place in the EU. Transcending the left–right divide – or more accurately voters' partisan affinities with the PS or Les Républicains – Macron united a well-off and well-educated electorate that perceives France's connections with the outside world in very positive terms, and does not want to risk any break with the European integration process. Since the election campaign – and in continuity with the PS's so-called 'modernizing' agenda[10] – Macron proclaimed his intention of using European unification as a lever to drive the complete transition of French capitalism towards a neoliberal model. His first actions in government could hardly have provided clearer confirmation of this. However, even within his electorate there is not unanimous support for neoliberal reforms. In this regard, it is interesting to compare the expectations of those who voted for Macron in the first round of the presidential election with those of the voters who opted for an LREM candidate in the first round of the legislative contest.

In the presidential election, Macron was the choice of voters who considered France's continued involvement in the EU a priority; conversely, the electorate who favoured neoliberal reforms was split between him and François Fillon. Thus, among voters who considered it necessary to cut the number of state employees, Fillon (32 per cent) beat Macron (23 per cent) by a wide margin. This was also the case, if less strikingly so, among voters who thought economic policy choices should prioritize businesses (Fillon, 33 per cent; Macron, 29 per cent),

---

9   Ifop, *Le tableau de bord de la transformation de la France* (May 2017).
10   See Chapter 2.

and above all among those who declared themselves opposed to state action to curb inequalities (Fillon, 39 per cent; Macron, 23 per cent).[11] Asked what they thought of reducing the number of state employees, only 10 per cent of Macron's voters said they 'agreed'; 39 per cent 'somewhat agreed', while the majority of the new president's electorate opposed such a measure (32 per cent 'somewhat disagreed' and 19 per cent 'disagreed').

However, Fillon's defeat and the deep crisis on the right, combined with the newly elected president's own policy announcements, soon produced a change in the new government's social base. This took place even in the few weeks between the presidential and legislative elections. We have already emphasized that LREM gathered a significant fraction of the right-wing electorate, especially among the self-employed. Thus, asked this same question about reducing the number of state employees, a large majority of the LREM electorate said they were in favour (16 per cent 'agreed', 42 per cent 'somewhat agreed'). Yet, even within the LREM electorate, which joined Macron's electoral base from the presidential election with a fraction of the right's base, neoliberal reforms were not unanimously supported: asked this same question, 28 per cent of LREM voters 'somewhat disagreed', and 14 per cent 'disagreed'.

Macron's project can thus be summarized as using the support of a social base united around continued European integration, in order to drive neoliberal reforms that are far from unanimously supported even within this same social base. It is thus only logical that his attempts to expand this new social alliance are directed more towards the right-wing (neo)liberal electorate – such as already took place in the brief period between the presidential and legislative elections.

MACRON'S STRATEGY: A STRENGTHENED TIE BETWEEN EU AND 'REFORMS'

It may seem more surprising that the new president should have chosen to embark upon neoliberal reforms at such a rapid pace right at the start of his term in office. Let us analyse the reasons for this.

---

11   All data from FES 2017.

Emmanuel Macron's presidential campaign began even while he was still economy minister, through the creation of networks of support – and especially the search for financial backing. But it was a relatively long time before he proposed any concrete electoral programme. When this programme did finally appear, in March 2017 – little over a month before the first round – it did contain some specific proposals, but it was mainly a set of very general objectives. This vagueness was not owed to any indecision on the candidate's part: in fact, revelations by Wikileaks indicate that his campaign team had studied sometimes very specific measures regarding some rather conflict-prone subjects, in liaison with 'experts' more or less internal to Macron's camp.[12]

If the detail of these measures was not disclosed to the electorate, it was easy enough to anticipate what the general orientation of Macron's actions would be if he became president. This could be deduced from France's economic, institutional and political dynamic since the early 1980s, and especially during Hollande's term, and indeed the new president's own personal career.[13] Having worked in the Finance Inspectorate before 'going private' at the Rothschild business bank from 2008 to 2012, he became secretary-general adjunct at the Élysée under Hollande (notably in charge of economic matters), and finally economy minister. He had also been the author of the *Rapport Attali*, commissioned by Nicolas Sarkozy at the beginning of his presidency.[14] This report recommended the 'en bloc' implementation of a series of neoliberal reforms in practically all domains, especially finance; the reforms proposed were not very original, but they were sometimes very radical. The practical enactment of these reforms was held up by the economic and financial crisis, which led Sarkozy to declare in his famous Toulon speech in September 2008 that the time for saying the market was always right had come to an end.

---

12   Emails exchanged between the members of Emmanuel Macron's campaign team and their correspondents, at wikileaks.org/macron-emails.

13   See Bruno Amable, *Structural Crisis and Institutional Change in Modern Capitalism: French Capitalism in Transition* (Oxford, Oxford University Press, 2017).

14   Jacques Attali, *Rapport de la Commission pour la libération de la croissance française* (Paris: XO Éditions, La Documentation française, 2008).

The *Rapport Attali* was just the latest avatar of a technocratic literature that had been in vogue since at least the early 2000s.[15] But what distinguished it from its many predecessors was its systematic character. In this sense, it gave valuable indications as to what could be expected from a Macron presidency: the pursuit of a radical project for the neoliberal transformation of the French socioeconomic model. This was a project of distant origins that gradually become the governmental right's main objective after the crisis of the 1970s – and then, with more ambiguities and difficulties, or even elements of reticence, that of the governmental left (the PS and its satellites) starting in the 1980s, especially after 2012.[16]

The freshly elected Macron would adopt, in his own way, the old refrain about France being 'impossible to reform'. As he put it, 'France is not a reformable country, it is a people that hates reforms. We need to propose that it deeply transform.'[17] We can compare this statement to that made by the leader of the right in 1984, when Jacques Chirac promised that, as soon as he was in office again, there would be a 'rather sharp' change of (socioeconomic) model. But unlike in the case of Chirac's return to power in 1986, in 2017 Macron could count on a five-year term in which he would enjoy an absolute majority (54 per cent) of MPs acting on his own command, and a weakened and divided social and political opposition.[18] Indeed, 5.7 per cent of seats in the National Assembly belonged to the left (France Insoumise + PCF), 5.3 per cent to the PS and its satellites, 8.1 to the centre-right (MoDem), 17.3 per cent to the conservative right (Les Républicains) and 1.4 per cent to the Front National.

The scale of Macron's ambitions, in terms of radically changing the model of French capitalism, was expressed in the number and diversity of the promised (or anticipated) areas of government business. These ranged from the pursuit of a 'reform' of employment relations to the

15   See Bruno Amable, 'Reforming Europe: Is the Third Way the Only Way?' *Prisme* 3 (Paris: Centre Cournot, 2004).

16   See Chapter 2.

17   Emmanuel Macron, Bucharest, 24 August 2017.

18   Many of Macron's MPs had no previous political experience, and owed almost everything to Emmanuel Macron personally.

'reform' of unemployment insurance and occupational training; from the alignment of special pension regimes to a generalized system (itself open to deep changes); from the 'reform' of the state rail company SNCF and the removal of railworkers' special status to the 'reform' of higher education, with the introduction of selection for university places, and the 'reform' of public services, with a drastic reduction of the number of general-status civil servants – and so on. Macron thus chose the tactic of all-out attack. In this, he was counting on the inability of the resistance in society to organize into a common front[19] – and on the either passive or active complicity of trade unions, competing to secure their place as the government's privileged interlocutor in negotiations. We may, moreover, note in passing that, while it was once commonplace to consider that the competition between trade unions led them to outbid each other in terms of advancing bolder demands, under the Hollande administration, and especially the early months of Macron's presidency, the opposite has been the case. The CFDT has long shown itself to be 'understanding' of neoliberal 'reform' plans; at the beginning of Macron's presidency, the FO union also fell in behind it.[20]

RESTORING PROFITABILITY

Emmanuel Macron's political marketing is always trumpeting his 'novelty'. Yet the orientation of his economic policy is anything but original. His policies pursue the modernist/neoliberal technocratic tradition embodied by Valéry Giscard d'Estaing since the 1960s. Indeed, they also follow in the wake of earlier attempts at a break with the French socioeconomic model inherited from the Fordist period, whether by Chirac in the 1980s, Balladur in the 1990s, Sarkozy in the 2000s or Hollande in the 2010s, all under the banner of 'reform'. His policies are also inspired by the recommendations of think tanks close to the neoliberal right and employers[21] – or, quite simply, by the Medef bosses' federation itself.

---

19 The so-called 'convergence of struggles' – the leitmotiv of the Nuit Debout movement in 2016 – seemed out of reach, at least as of spring 2018.

20 Note the CFDT's very 'conciliatory' attitude towards the 1995 social security reform, which gave rise to a social movement bigger than any other since May 1968.

21 Such as the Institut Montaigne or the Institut de l'Entreprise.

Picking up, after so many others, on the so-called 'Schmidt theorem',[22] part of these 'reforms' are devoted to helping out capital by increasing firms' profit margins, and more generally increasing profitability. These measures' consequences in terms of inequality – the rise of which has ended up worrying even the economists who could least be suspected of excessive concern for the social question[23] – are openly accepted, at least in part. Here we see the deployment of 'trickle down' (pseudo-)theory[24] – though Macron prefers to re-baptize it as the theory of the 'lead climber'.[25] The epithet calling him the 'president of the rich' spread rapidly – and not without reason.

We should, moreover, set this acceptance (or even promotion) of inequalities within a wider context. Macron's 'reforms' doubtless have the more or less direct consequence of increasing inequalities of income and status (through the precaritization of part of the waged workforce). We should not consider these consequences as unfortunate side-effects. They are something the Macron camp has resigned itself to – as if unwillingly – in the name of the imperatives of the 'reform', hoping that they will fade once 'fresh growth' arrives. From the viewpoint of the constitution and the consolidation of a dominant bourgeois bloc, these inequalities in fact fulfil a crucial function, because they help break the old bonds of solidarity that kept certain socioeconomic categories in either the left- or right-wing bloc. They encourage the break-up of the old blocs and make possible – if not certain – the reaggregation of certain social groups within the bourgeois bloc. But, as we shall see, they also carry risks concerning the sustainability of the bourgeois bloc itself.

---

22   Today's profits make for tomorrow's investment and the jobs of the day after tomorrow.

23   The OECD and IMF have made this theme one of their main concerns. They have devoted numerous publications to drawing attention to the negative consequences of rising inequality – a rise that can be observed in all countries, to different degrees.

24   As popularized by Ronald Reagan, who claimed that making the rich richer would end up benefiting the poor. This idea had already emerged in the eighteenth-century *querelle du luxe* and in Mandeville's fable of the bees.

25   'I believe in the lead climber, there are men and women who succeed because they are talented, I want us to celebrate them … If we start chucking pebbles at the lead climber, then the whole line will come crashing down.' Emmanuel Macron, interview with TF1-LCI, 15 October 2017.

SO-CALLED 'NEW GROWTH'

For the group of economists who supported Macron's candidacy, he was 'the most able to lay the foundations of new economic growth ... because he chooses to bet on work, youth, innovation, inclusion, investment and the ecological transition.'[26] The rhetoric of 'new growth' is a vehicle for a whole set of ideas that can easily be compared to the neoliberal vision of an economy constantly being shaken up by heroic entrepreneurs.[27] In this view, the latter ask only to be free of regulatory barriers, so that they can continue doing battle in a context of hard-fought but honest competition. This permanent change requires individuals who are able to adapt easily to the new conditions of competition and employability: this itself points back to the need for 'flexibility', which – thanks to the abolition of the supposedly undue protections that 'insiders' are said to enjoy at the expense of 'outsiders' – is also taken for a guarantee of 'inclusiveness'. Another typically neoliberal theme is the distinction between (good) profits, which reward the most deserving – those who take risks and innovate – and (bad) rents. This reasoning resurfaced during the debates over the elimination of the wealth tax.

The primary importance attributed to innovation is expressed in the use of the slogan 'start-up nation'.[28] This phrase betrays a belief in what Mariana Mazzucato, an economist specializing in technological change, calls the Silicon Valley myth.[29] This myth is based on the idea that growth comes only from small innovative firms, ignoring the crucial role that public research and infrastructure play in the innovation process. Moreover, the obsession with 'innovation' as the unique source of technological progress hides the fact that productivity gains more often result from improvements that already-established firms

---

26   'Pourquoi nous soutenons Emmanuel Macron', column on *Le Monde*'s website, 12 April 2017.

27   See Chapter 2.

28   The expression was used by Macron in June 2017 as he opened Station F, the campus and giant 'incubator' created by Free's owner Xavier Niel. This term was originally used to characterize the Israeli economy. Dan Senor and Saul Singer, *Start-up Nation: The Story of Israel's Economic Miracle* (New York: Twelve, 2011).

29   Mariana Mazzucato, *The Entrepreneurial State: Debunking Public vs. Private Sector Myths* (London: Anthem, 2014).

make to existing products and techniques, rather than from 'creative destruction'[30]

In connection with the emphasis on the permanent shake-ups in the economy owing to innovation, the Macron camp's rhetoric emphasizes the central role of education and training – a consequence of individuals' constant need to adapt in order to find employment.[31] As noted in Chapter Two, this is a central element of the original neoliberalism – a vision of society and the economy already expressed by Walter Lippmann.[32] It thus constantly trots out the idea of the end of stable careers. The individual must now change jobs several times during their career, thus implying a continual, 'lifelong' training process.

The first measures taken under Macron's presidency pursued the 'reform' of employment relations. This was consistent with the above-described conception of the social dynamic – and also stood in continuity with the Loi Travail, passed under Hollande's presidency. As with the El Khomri bill (named after Labour Minister Myriam El Khomri), the flexibilization measures were justified in terms of the alleged need to reassure employers who might hesitate to hire staff because they feared not being able to lay them off if the economic situation worsened. The economic risk – in the liberal vision, the very source of profit's legitimacy[33] – is thus offloaded onto the worker, who must find some means of securing employment elsewhere, through training.

'REFORMS' TO SUIT EUROPE (OR THE OPPOSITE)?

Alongside 'reforms', the other central dimension of Macron's policy is the pursuit and deepening of European integration. This is unsurprising; as we have repeatedly emphasized in this book, ever since the

---

30 Daniel Garcia-Macia, Chang-Tai Hsieh and Peter J. Klenow, *How Destructive is Innovation?*, NBER Working Paper No. 22953 (2016).

31 This idea is encapsulated in a 15 October 2017 tweet by Emmanuel Macron addressed to the French people, 'Society is changing: I want to arm you to find your place in this change, rather than pretend to protect you against it.' Another tweet, on 28 March 2018 specifies: 'We should not fear and reject change. It is everywhere at work and it can guide us for the better.'

32 Walter Lippmann, *The Good Society* (Boston, MA: Little, Brown, 1937).

33 Frank Knight's perspective, for example.

1980s the European project has been used in France to legitimize institutional changes that work in the direction of the neoliberal model. The
post-election survey data we cited above, moreover, show that Macron
built his social base and electoral success around support for French
involvement in the EU. Indeed, Macron explicitly links the European question to the supposed need for 'reforms'. In his explanation,
France is making 'indispensable reforms' in order to secure Germany's
'restored confidence'; in this climate of renewed trust, Germany will,
he claims, agree to loosen the constraints weighing down macroeconomic policy, and allow the deepening of European integration in the
direction of fiscal federalism.

This approach supposes that the ruling coalition in Germany
will not adopt a hard line on respecting European budget treaties.
From this point of view, Macron has been lucky – if perhaps not lucky
enough. After the German elections in autumn 2017, the possibility
emerged of a CDU/CSU–FDP–Green coalition. Considering the FDP's
very tough positions on the European question, such a coalition would
have been highly unfavourable to Macron's plans. But the FDP's pre-
varication led this project to collapse, and in spring 2018 a new 'grand
coalition' of the CDU/CSU and the SPD finally saw the light of day. Yet
the delays caused by the SPD's hesitation and about-turns have prevented Macron from making progress on Eurozone reform. In general,
political developments in Germany – including the weakening of the
traditional parties of government and the rise of the AfD – represent
a potential threat to the properly European dimension of Macron's
policy. Moreover, this policy should not be mistaken for any grand
plan for the 'refoundation' of the Eurozone – it is, rather, a series of
alterations to existing mechanisms, without crossing the red lines
that Germany has drawn. (Hence, no mutualization of public debts,
no permanent transfers between states, and no automatic reciprocal-
aid mechanisms while there remains the condition that 'reforms' be
implemented, and so on).

THE START OF MACRON'S TERM: SETTING COURSE
TOWARD THE NEOLIBERAL MODEL

The First Budget

The tactic Macron adopted was to take advantage of LREM's absolute majority in the National Assembly to string together a series of measures that, under other presidents, would each have prompted significant social opposition. The nice surprise for Macron's camp was that the all-out attack against the French socioeconomic model sparked only very weak opposition – by spring 2018, at least – in particular from the unions, which remained divided and marked by internecine rivalry.

The Macron presidency's first budget, in 2018, combined a considerable fall in public spending (social housing, healthcare) with a tax cut mainly concentrated on capital gains, high incomes and a rise in Generalized Social Contribution (CSG) contributions. The net balance sheet of this operation is, at first glance, a relatively neutral effect on households' purchasing power – but it is strongly differentiated according to income and asset levels.[34] Well-off households are most advantaged: the OFCE thus estimates that the 2 per cent at the very top of the income scale, who hold the greater part of real-estate capital, will rake in most of the gains to be had from the reform. Conversely, the poorest households are set to lose most, since rises in indirect taxation will not be fully offset by the rise in minimum thresholds. Overall, the operation should have a neutral effect on the middle classes. We thus see that the first budget of the Macron presidency is marked by a strong bias in favour of well-off households.

Decrees

We should not forget that, under Hollande's presidency, Macron himself ought to have tabled the Loi Travail, which was instead

---

34   Pierre Madec, Mathieu Plane and Raul Sampognaro, *Budget 2018: pas d'austérité mais des inégalités*, OFCE Policy Brief 30 (2018).

ultimately allocated to another minister, Myriam El Khomri. The decrees reforming the labour code are a continuation of this earlier bill. Its overall logic is to lower the cost of sackings to employers' advantage: it makes this process automatic, imposes limits on the recourse to judges (ombudsmen), fixes a scale of compensation, reduces the time-frame for legal appeals, and provides a form letter for firing a worker. Like those around the Loi Travail, the debates surrounding Macron's decrees showed that a non-negligible share of economists, including mainstream ones, doubt the relevance of this type of measure in reducing unemployment. The prime minister even admitted that 'by no means' was employment law the main cause of unemployment.

Macron's decrees built on the El Khomri bill (and, in a certain sense, on Fillon's 2004 bill and his 2007 'social dialogue modernization' bill)[35] in challenging the hierarchy of norms. That is, these reforms give priority to company-level agreements over industry-level ones, and authorize these agreements to define questions that once pertained to the field of law. The obvious logic of these normative changes is a weakening of workers' bargaining power. Paradoxically, from a liberal point of view, a company-level agreement can change an individual's work contract: salary levels, the 'modulation' of working time, the imposition of geographical or professional 'mobility', and even (for managers) a calculation of working time in terms of days per year rather than hours per week.

The El Khomri bill had already asserted that the Labour Code had to be re-founded on a few core principles. It held that employment relations would henceforth essentially be regulated not by law but by negotiation at the level of the firm – or even a given branch of industry, in the absence of any decentralized agreement. In this logic, the law is reduced to a residual role, as a palliative for the possible absence of agreements at a lower level. The Labour Code was supposed to be rewritten by a commission over two years, though this became redundant when Macron issued his decrees. The process of rewriting the code, which could already have been pushed through quickly with the mechanisms stipulated in the Loi Travail, was further accelerated

---

35   See Bruno Amable, 'The Political Economy of Neo-Liberal Interventionism in French Industrial Relations', *ILR Review* 69: 3 (2016).

by these decrees. These increased the role of individual branches of industry, but only to substitute them for the legislator (in terms of alterations to working time, fixed-length contracts, new 'worksite' contracts, trial periods, and so on). We know, moreover, that the plan was to drastically cut the number of branches recognized (from over 800 to fewer than 100). We should also remember that the measures taken through the decrees include the changing of the geographical perimeter taken into consideration to evaluate an international company's economic difficulties and its need to defend its competitiveness – a perimeter now drawn around France and not the group as a whole. This makes it possible for a firm that is in rude financial health to use a little creative accounting to push its French affiliate into the red, and thus justify the outsourcing and lay-offs it wanted to carry out anyway. Moreover, the rules for evaluating the formal legality of a firing have been loosened (for instance, in terms of providing a reason in the termination letter). The decrees also respond to an old demand of the employers' organizations: the bodies that represent workers within the firm – the Enterprise Committee (CE), the Personnel Delegates (DP) and the Committee for Health, Safety and Working Conditions (CHSCT) – are all merged. The effect of this measure will be to reduce the number of staff representatives. This will cause no lack of problems for unions (and workers), who will see their local-level representation in firms weakened.

The Reform to Unemployment Insurance

The unions also dreaded Macron's reform to unemployment insurance. In the election campaign, he had promised to establish a 'universal unemployment' system including the self-employed and people who had voluntarily quit their jobs. Such an extension of unemployment coverage necessarily had to involve a change to the compensation itself. The insurance system, managed by the social partners and founded on the *right* to compensation for those who have paid in, logically had to change into what he called a system 'drastically' set under control by the public authorities, and – we can easily deduce – one less generous than had existed previously.

The first aspect of this reform is the change to how it was financed. The contributions drawn from wages were abolished and replaced by a tax levied on all incomes through the Generalised Social Contribution (CSG), which breaks the logic that attaches contribution to the right to compensation. Ultimately, workers – or their representatives – are thus destined to lose their role in managing the unemployment compensation system. If they are no longer the ones financing the system, what right would they have to manage it? So, it was no surprise that the bill tabled with the State Council in late March 2018 planned to strengthen the state's role in determining the terms of compensation. The governance of the unemployment insurance system had to be altered so as to provide the framework for discussions between unions and employers. This especially concerned the system's financial prospects over time and the rules for compensation – including the possibility of building up a future unemployment benefit through income from labour. The system in place until the reform had indexed benefit payments to the previously received wage, which also served as the basis for calculating the contributions made. The break in the link between contributions and compensation instead opened the door to a potentially very ungenerous flat-rate compensation system like the one operating in the United Kingdom. This makes it all the more likely that the financing of the universal system sought by Macron will almost automatically bring a fall in compensation levels.

The second aspect of this reform was the intensified control of the unemployed. During his presidential campaign, Macron insisted that unemployed people who refused a 'reasonable' job offer should be barred from receiving payments. Here, he was adopting a traditional theme of the right. In fact, the increased pressure on the unemployed was not so much a legal problem – they could already be deprived of benefits if they refused a job offer – as an organizational one: Who decides that the offer is 'reasonable', and thus that someone should be barred from receiving compensation? The spring 2018 bill stipulated that it would now be the prerogative of the advisor at jobs agency Pôle emploi, who would make their judgement on the basis of the 'local economic context' – or, as the unions had it, 'according to the needs of the local bosses'.

The 'President of the Rich'

The change in the tax system in favour of those who hold capital has translated into several measures. The Solidarity Tax on Wealth (ISF) has been replaced by a single flat-rate payment (PFU) on incomes from movable assets, as well as a wealth tax on real estate (IFI). This reform advantages the best-off households, which own the greater part of moveable capital, and may penalize part of the middle classes, whose wealth is essentially in real estate.[36] Contrary to what Macron promised during the election campaign, this reform has translated into a fall in receipts for the state budget. This is, indeed, a transfer of resources towards the richest, and has led the opposition on the left to refer to Macron as the 'president of the rich'.[37]

Added to this 'reform' of ISF is the fall in taxes on firms: a cut in business taxes, a one-point rise in the Tax Credit for Competitiveness and Employment (CICE) and the elimination of the contribution on dividends. Conversely, households will have to pay more, with increased indirect taxes on tobacco and fossil fuels and the hike in the CSG, which is not fully offset by the reduction in the amount of contributions drawn directly from pay packets. This latter change in any case only benefits those receiving wages, while penalizing the retired in particular. If it is possible (according to what theories of the political-economic cycle tell us) that the burden on households will gradually fall over the course of Macron's term, the beginning of his presidency has certainly been inspired by the will to favour capital and by the improbable conclusions of 'trickle-down theory'.

The lowest-income households will also suffer the reduction (in several stages) of Personalised Housing Alliance (APL). Backed by some economic studies that tended to show that APL was largely, or even entirely, captured by landlords through rent increases, the government presented its reduction as a fight against unearned incomes and a neutral measure for tenants. But if part of the APL has ended up

---

36   According to Madec, Plane and Sampognaro, *Budget 2018*, 42 per cent of all the tax gains will be made by the richest 5 per cent of households.

37   The reform is in fact the abolition of a measure taken under the first government of Hollande's presidency, returning to the situation that existed when the right was in power.

in the hands of landlords, it is also a way of subsidizing social housing. The fall in APL, offset by a fall in rents, would thus lead to a cut in the resources for this sector (of the order of 45 euros per monthly payment), even as other subsidies – which, by the same logic, will end up in the pockets of private landlords and property developers – are not affected.

Privatization and Reform in the SNCF

It is impossible to imagine a neoliberal economic programme without privatizations.[38] Logically enough, Macron's programme includes €10 billion worth of them. This high figure poses questions (and they are not difficult to answer) over the possibility that the French style of public services will survive. After the great waves of privatizations in the 1980s and 1990s, all that is left in the sector are 'traditional' public services (network industries, communications, transport, energy) and strategic companies. The sale of the state's share in private companies (for example, Renault, PSA, Air France and Orange) could not reach the planned total amount – and it would also put in doubt the possibility of defining an industrial policy in the sectors concerned. Eventually, La Poste or Engie (formerly Gaz de France) could also be affected.

In line with expectations, in spring 2018 the government announced the privatization of Aéroports de Paris (the public share in AdP amounted to €7 billion in early 2018) and the Française des Jeux gambling company. This has raised question marks even within the president's parliamentary cohort. Indeed, as well as being a strategic industry, the airports (like gambling) are a profitable business, a source of receipts for the state coffers. Selling them to the private sector is thus hard to justify in terms of the 'sound management' of the public finances.[39]

---

38   The measures supposed to encourage competition by reducing regulation in the markets for the goods and services most often translate into a dismantling of public services, to the advantage of new, private monopolies that have all too little to do with the charming story of the innovative little firm. Its supposedly positive impact on growth is also illusory. See Bruno Amable and Ivan Ledezma, *Libéralisation, innovation et croissance. Faut-il vraiment les associer?* (Paris: Ed. Rue d'Ulm, 2016).

39   Especially as an unfortunate precedent ought to serve as a caution. In 2015, 49.99

As if blind to the very strong growth of public criticism in the country that took the lead in rail privatization – the United Kingdom – in spring 2018 the Macron presidency's plans in this field took on almost Thatcherite dimensions.[40] Following a classic procedure, a 2018 government-commissioned report put together by none other than former Air France CEO Jean-Cyril Spinetta issued a series of recommendations supposed to inspire future reforms. The report spoke of the end of SNCF's role as a public service and its opening up to competition through its transformation into a limited company; this would entail the abolition of the railworkers' special status, the breaking-up of the network's management,[41] and the branching-off of its passenger and freight businesses. As is so often the case, European integration served as a basis for these recommendations. The opening up of rail to competition had indeed been stipulated for 2019, and the SNCF's public status could be seen by the Brussels authorities as a distortion of competition. This should obviously be tied to the fact that the various French governments have never done anything to ensure that European treaties recognize its (French-style) status as a public service.

The abolition of the railworkers' special status is more political than economic in character. This status does not cost much, considering the expected profitability of a privatised SNCF. Some even think that abolishing this status will be more expensive than keeping it.[42] But, from a political point of view, the decision to abolish it has allowed for a tug-of-war with a particularly combative group of workers, the force behind the defeat of the Juppé plan to reform social protection back in 1995. Winning a victory over the railworkers in spring

---

per cent of Toulouse Airport was sold to a Chinese consortium chosen by then economy minister, Emmanuel Macron. The state's intention was to sell the rest of its shares to this group at a later stage. But it had to abandon this plan in February 2018 because of the Chinese shareholder's predatory behaviour and the protests – especially by local elected officials – that resulted.

40   In the United Kingdom the management and maintenance of the network came back into public hands in 2014, but all other aspects of the railways are operated under franchise by private companies, which also receive public subsidies. Privatization has brought a spectacular rise in ticket prices, combined with frequent delays and cancellations in certain parts of the country.

41   Though, as we have seen, in 2014 the UK mounted a reversal in this regard.

42   Samuel Chalom, 'La suppression du statut des cheminots pourrait coûter plus cher que son maintien', *Capital*, 18 March 2018.

2018 – overcoming the obstacle that previous 'reform' attempts crashed against – could have a decisive symbolic value, which would ease the success of the rest of the 'reform' plan over the rest of Macron's presidency.

Towards Selection for University Places

During his campaign, education was one of Macron's stated priorities. It is advanced as a solution to all problems of employability, and as completely indispensable to policies favouring capital (the innovative entrepreneuriat). In the field of higher education, the plans of prime minister Édouard Philippe's government and education minister Jean-Michel Blanquer seem less orientated towards the future than towards old obsessions of right-wingers within the universities: above all selection for places, a theme that thirty years previously killed off the last attempt at a sharp change to the French model.[43] In this new law's logic (out of concern for speedy implementation, it was applied before it had even been voted on), students will be directed towards courses where they may be accepted, if there is room for them. This implies a questioning of the right to university access, which had previously been conditional only on the achievement of a secondary-school leaving certificate, the baccalauréat – itself the object of a reform that seeks to grant a more important place to ongoing control of students' progress, thus increasing universities' ability to evaluate candidates who want to study with them. It seems that the most direct effect of the reform will be to allow the most in-demand establishments and courses not to accept students they do not want – typically, ones from the popular classes. This is thus likely to have a major impact on the reproduction of social inequalities.

---

43   In 1986 the Loi Devaquet, an attempt to reform the teaching system in higher education, met with strong opposition among students. Chirac's government realized the danger that this resistance would join forces with the December 1986 railworkers' strikes, and, after one student protestor was killed, it preferred to withdraw the bill. This failure would have further consequences at the following presidential election, in 1988, where Chirac lost to Mitterrand.

Opposition Forces at a Strategic Impasse

Macron was lifted into power by a new social alliance that would be 'beyond left and right' or, more accurately, 'of both left and right'. It unites well-off categories with high qualification levels in an alliance built around support for European integration. The first measures of his presidency, which we have just surveyed, leave no doubt as to what Macron's project is: he intends to use the European question as a lever to carry through an institutional programme for the full-scale reform of French capitalism towards a neoliberal model. The new government is thus relying on a minoritarian but relatively coherent social bloc, as it pursues a clearly identified goal. To his great advantage, Macron's government is confronted with political adversaries who are themselves going through strategic crises; these crises differ in intensity, but it is difficult to find a solution to any of them.

Macron is enacting a project of social and economic transformation that the right has been unsuccessfully trying to complete for four decades. Indeed, in finding an original solution to the problem France's conservative parties have for so long posed themselves, Macron has confronted them with a dilemma: they can either rally behind LREM, or choose the path of radicalization and seek an alliance with the FN.

The left, for its part, has been definitively cut off from a part of its social bloc. The alliance, both political and social, that it was able to build under the Fifth Republic seems to have broken up for good over the question of European integration and the maintenance of the French social model. The reconstitution of a left-wing bloc does not collide with the question of how to elaborate a suitable political strategy, but also – perhaps most importantly – with the institutional constraints carved in stone in the European treaties. These constraints make it difficult, perhaps impossible, to resolve the contradiction between European integration and a 'non-neoliberal' social and economic model. The defeat of the PS, which long campaigned in European elections on the theme of 'a social Europe', is a striking example of the difficulty in reconciling two such radically opposed elements.

The Crisis of the Old 'Governmental' Parties

We should note at this point that the crisis of the social alliances that used to support the 'governmental' left and right – something we have dwelled on at length in previous chapters – has now become a self-evident reality. The rout suffered by the Parti Socialiste, today threatened with extinction, is so blatant that it merits no further attention: the reader can refer to Chapter 2 to understand how it began. But when we analyse François Fillon's result in the first round of the 2017 presidential election, we see that the right is also undergoing a profound crisis. The Républicains' candidate inherited quite a small share of the vote that Sarkozy had taken in 2012: only three in five of his voters chose to stay loyal to the main party of the governmental right. Worse, in the absence of a candidate for the traditional centrist party UDF/MoDem, Fillon picked up only 18 per cent of the voters who had backed François Bayrou five years previously; and, despite a campaign centred on the themes of economic liberalism and conservative values, he captured only 8 per cent of Le Pen's 2012 electorate. But it is the vote breakdown by social-occupational group that gives a real measure of the right's failure to provide a convincing perspective for government. Indeed, more than half (52 per cent) of Fillon's electorate in the presidential election was made up of pensioners, and almost two-thirds (62 per cent) were economically inactive. The only socio-occupational group in which Fillon surpassed his average score nationally, other than pensioners (among whom he took 34 per cent support), was the self-employed (25 per cent): and, as we have stressed, this category rapidly joined the new government's electoral base at the legislative elections that followed just weeks later.[44] In these latter elections, pensioners made up some 60 per cent of Les Républicains' electorate.[45]

The disintegration of the social alliances on both right and left is thus no longer in doubt. But we should question whether the new divide on which Macron relies will itself be able to restructure the political battle-lines in France. We should note that, whatever the rhetoric

---

44   Ifop (2017P).
45   Ifop (2017L).

of the government and the dominant media outlets, Macron did not build his victory around the defence of an 'open society'; we need only consider his handling of immigration or the policing response to social movements to dispel any vision inspired by propaganda rather than analysis.[46] Macron based his rise to power on the guarantee of strong continuity in the European integration process; his project is to consolidate an alliance prepared to support a vast programme of neoliberal reforms in the name of guaranteeing the viability of the EU.

The hypothetical new axis of political differentiation would therefore set up an opposition between (a) well-off voters in favour of EU integration and neoliberal reforms and (b) the popular-classes, themselves rallied 'beyond left and right' around the re-establishment of France's economic borders and the defence of the peculiarities of French capitalism. If Macron has occupied the first pole of this axis, an analysis of the election results confirms the doubts we have expressed here regarding the possibility of making the opposite pole into an actual political force. The likely insurmountable obstacle to the articulation of any political offer seeking the support of the popular classes as a whole lies in the deep contradictions running through their various expectations. Very telling in this regard is the defeat of the Front National. It explicitly proposed – at least as far as the component most identified with Marine Le Pen's campaign is concerned – to unite the popular classes around a nationalist perspective. But an analysis of the result for Jean-Luc Mélenchon – who at certain moments in his campaign expressed a desire to transcend the political left's old boundaries and build an alliance around economic patriotism – also indicates that an effective opposition to the new government cannot escape the traditional left–right divide.

---

46   In a column for *Le Monde* published on 2 January 2017, Emmanuel Macron wrote: 'Chancellor Merkel and German society as a whole have been up to the level of our shared values; they have saved our collective dignity by welcoming refugees in distress.' The tone would radically change once Macron reached power. A November 2017 circular enjoined police to take speedy action to expel failed asylum seekers. The police's very aggressive behaviour (tearing tents and sleeping bags, systematic use of tear gas) seemed to correspond to the executive's apparent desire to dissuade immigrants and refugees from staying in France. This sheds particular light on Macron's July 2017 statement that 'by the end of this year I want there to be no more men and women in the streets, in the woods'. The 'asylum and immigration' bill heralded a fresh repressive turn in spring 2018.

The FN's Defeat and the Difficulty of Uniting an Anti-EU Alliance

In emphasising economic sovereigntism and the perspective of a rupture with the European Union, Marine Le Pen united a popular-class electorate that considers itself penalized by the opening of markets to international competition. Only 8 per cent of her first-round voters counted themselves among the 'winners and beneficiaries of globalization', whereas 68 per cent perceived themselves as the 'losers and victims' of this process.[47] She achieved remarkable scores among voters whose educational qualification levels fall short of the *baccalauréat* (30 per cent in the first round) and among those whose household income is less than €1,250 a month (32 per cent).[48] A large proportion of her voters (78 per cent) think that France should 'protect itself from the world more',[49] and 67 per cent think that France's EU membership is 'mostly a bad thing'.[50]

But it would be mistaken to take these data as sufficient proof that, in the new political space, Marine Le Pen has succeeded in occupying the pole opposite to Macron's.[51] In reality, the attempt to give the Front National a new social base – a project that sought to build an alliance rearticulating the popular-class fractions of the old left- and right-wing blocs – has translated into a failure. The data show that the FN electorate has evolved very little compared to 2012: Marine Le Pen took 80 per cent of her vote from an electorate that had already backed her five years previously, 14 per cent from previous Sarkozy voters, and only 6 per cent from those who had delivered Hollande into first place in the opening round of the 2012 contest. But the politically most important shift is that regarding the transfer of voters from Mélenchon in 2012 to Le Pen in 2017. After all, the Front de Gauche candidate had won the support of a large share of the popular classes – the same electorate that Le Pen wanted to unite behind her own candidacy. Yet a measure of the Front National's strategic failure was the fact that only 4 per cent

---

47   Ifop (2017P).

48   Ipsos, *1er tour.*

49   Cevipof: 'Mondialisation, protectionnisme et recomposition, L'enquête électorale française: comprendre 2017', wave 14, June 2017.

50   Ifop, *Ce que veulent les Français – Volet 2.*

51   The source for Fig. 5.4 is Ipsos, *1er tour*; for Fig. 5.5, Cevipof, 'Mondialisation, protectionnisme et recomposition.'

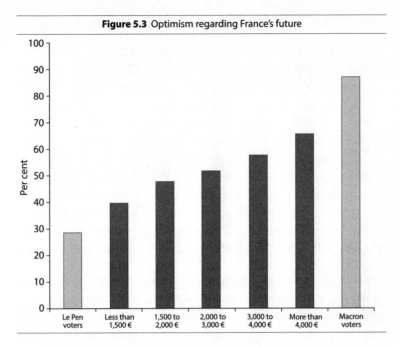

Figure 5.3 Optimism regarding France's future

of 2012 Mélenchon voters opted for Le Pen in the 2017 presidential elections (and since Mélenchon had taken 11.1 per cent in that contest, this corresponded to under 0.5 per cent of the overall electorate).[52] Marine Le Pen thus failed to transcend the left–right divide: the fact that she reached the second round was owed to the support of voters who positioned themselves on the right (24 per cent of whom voted for her) and the far-right (80 per cent,) while she obtained only 2 per cent among voters who position themselves on the left.[53]

The other dimension of the Front National's failure is linked to the split between its voters' expectations and the position it would have had to adopt according to the strategy driven by figures like Florian Philippot (tellingly, after the election, he quit the party). As we have indicated, this strategy, which was indeed Le Pen's strategy for much of the campaign, sought to build an oppositional pole on the same axis as the bourgeois bloc, but from the opposite side. This would have meant a nationalist pole, hostile to the European Union and the single

---

52   Ifop (2017P).
53   Ipsos, *1er tour*.

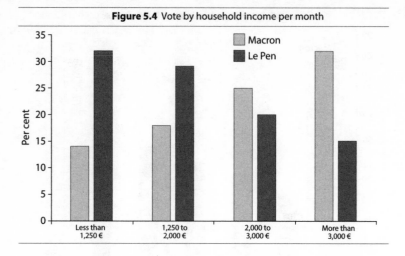

Figure 5.4 Vote by household income per month

currency, and in favour of maintaining certain peculiarities of French capitalism, with which the popular classes as a whole supposedly identified. In truth, though, the Front National's base was profoundly split over the question of 'reforms'. For example, 64 per cent of Le Pen's electorate supported the inversion of the hierarchy of norms between company-level and industrial-level negotiations: 53 per cent agreed that an upper ceiling should be set on compensation for workers fired without just or serious cause.[54] Moreover, Le Pen achieved far from negligible scores among voters who demanded cuts in the number of state employees (20 per cent) and those who said they were hostile to state action to reduce inequalities (18 per cent).[55] The *frontiste* electorate is deeply split on economic questions: a questionnaire the FN itself distributed directly among 27,000 of its members tells us as much.[56] For example, 47 per cent of its members support the thirty-five-hour working week, while 39 per cent are opposed; 41 per cent back state-sponsored jobs (*contrats aidés*) but 42 per cent are against; a third (33 per cent) approve the abolition of the Solidarity Tax on Wealth, and a large majority (71 per cent) demand a reduction in the number of

---

54   Ifop, *Les Français et la réforme du code du travail*, July 2017.

55   FES 2017.

56   The survey results were published on the FN's official Facebook page on 10 March 2018. See also Guillaume de Calignon 'Les questions économiques divisent les militants du FN', *Les Echos*, 11 March 2018.

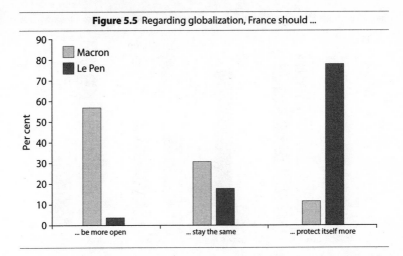

Figure 5.5 Regarding globalization, France should ...

local- and regional-level officials. Here, therefore, we are very far from a social alliance that is ready to take up the struggle against the reforms in the new government's economic programme.

The collapse in FN support between the presidential election (21.4 per cent for Le Pen in the first round) and the legislative contest (13.2 per cent for the FN in the first round) is also linked to shifts in the voting patterns of white-collar workers (down from 30 to 16 per cent), self-employed workers (from 19 to 10 per cent) and also blue-collar workers (from 39 to 31 per cent) – another sign that the 'sovereigntist' pact among the popular classes, as imagined by some FN leaders, has not worked.[57] This failure revived the latent conflict between the two opposed elements within FN ranks: the neo- or ultra-liberal faction, which stands in continuity with the FN of the 1980s, and the one led by Florian Philippot, which wanted to ally a social orientation with a nationalist stance. The changed orientation of the FN's economic policy, which no longer seeks to exit the euro but to 'reform Europe' from within (like Macron!), signalled the victory of this first faction over the social/anti-EU one.[58]

---

57   Ifop (2017P); Ifop (2017L).

58   We might consider that, in light of the political balances within the EU, the project of building a 'Europe of nationalisms' of neoliberal orientation has a much greater chance of success than does a 'social Europe'.

Figure 5.6 Choice for president among voters whose household income allows them to cope ...

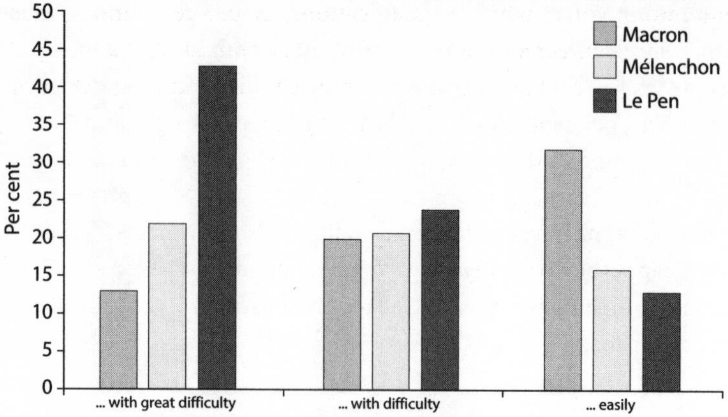

JEAN-LUC MÉLENCHON'S FRANCE INSOUMISE: NEW SOCIAL
ALLIANCE OR RENEWED COMPROMISE ON THE LEFT?

Jean-Luc Mélenchon achieved a remarkable score in the first round of
the presidential election (19.6 per cent) – a result that is all the more
promising given that his vote was anchored among younger generations.[59] The most important effect of this result is that it put an end to
the Parti Socialiste's hegemony over the left. At the same time, Mélenchon's electoral base remains strongly rooted in the space defined by
the old left-wing bloc – a reality that is partly at odds with a campaign
fought in the name of the 'people', in which red flags were replaced
by the *tricolore*.[60] Just 16 per cent of Mélenchon's voters said they had
no partisan preference, whereas 77 per cent said they were left-wing;
and it is worth emphasizing that only 4 per cent of Marine Le Pen's
2012 voters (0.7 per cent of the whole electorate) opted for the France
Insoumise candidate five years later.[61] From the social point of view,

---

59   Mélenchon scored 29 per cent among eighteen-to-twenty-four-year-olds, 24 per
cent among twenty-five-to-thirty-four-year-olds, and only 12 per cent among over-sixty-
fives. Ifop (2017P).

60   This is only somewhat paradoxical. France Insoumise's electoral campaign
was influenced by the works of Ernesto Laclau and Chantal Mouffe, who call for a *left*-
populism.

61   Ifop (2017P).

Mélenchon's electoral base was strongly inter-classist: he took 20 per cent among voters without qualifications, 22 per cent among those with a *baccalauréat* and 18 per cent of those with at least a bac + 2.[62] He took 25 per cent among those on household incomes under €1,250 a month, 23 per cent among those earning between €1,250 and €2,000, 18 per cent among those between €2,000 and €3,000, and 16 per cent among those earning more than €3,000.[63] Such electoral support across different levels of financial wellbeing shows that Mélenchon's vote escapes the divide between the popular and privileged classes – a cleavage which does, conversely, strongly separate Le Pen's social base from Macron's.

Result among Voters Whose Household Income Allows Them to Get By (With Great Difficulty, With Difficulty, Easily)

Looking beyond campaign rhetoric, these data allow us to say that Mélenchon's breakthrough was connected to his capacity to build a renewed left-wing compromise.[64] Before its crisis and then decomposition, the left-wing bloc had corresponded to an inter-class social alliance with which the waged fraction of the popular classes and the fraction of the bourgeois classes linked to intellectual professions and the public sector each identified.[65] Similarly, Mélenchon was supported by a significant share of blue-collar workers (25 per cent) and white-collar employees (24 per cent), but also among intermediate professions (26 per cent) and even managers and top professionals (16 per cent).

The good news is that Mélenchon was able to draw significant support among the popular-class categories who had deserted the left-wing camp en masse over many years. The bad news is that his social base is much more limited than the old left-wing bloc. Indeed, we should remember that, despite the France Insoumise candidate's result, in the presidential election the left suffered a major reversal: the Parti Socialiste lost some 9 million votes compared to 2012, whereas

---

62 Ibid.
63 Ipsos, *1er tour*.
64 The source for Fig. 5.6 is Ipsos, *1er tour*.
65 See the analysis in Chapter 1, pp. 14–17.

Mélenchon gained 3 million – representing a net loss of 6 million for the left. Taken together, the left-wing candidates collected 27 per cent of the vote, a historically low level – some sixteen points below what they had taken in the previous presidential election. The collapse at the first round of the legislative elections was even more drastic: compared to the Front de Gauche's performance in 2012, France Insoumise and the Parti Communiste advanced by seven points, but the PS and its allies dropped by over thirty points. And, while the total number of Insoumis and Communist MPs was seventeen higher than the Front de Gauche had had in the outgoing parliament, the PS and its allies lost a total of 286 seats.

An optimistic reading of Mélenchon's result would show this as the beginning of the rebuilding of a left-wing social alliance. A pessimist would identify his electorate as a residual aggregation of what remains of the left-wing bloc after it has already exploded. In either case, it is worth emphasizing that the contradictions that led to the crisis of the left are still present within France Insoumise's own electorate – and they risk blocking its own possible rise. As we have insisted throughout this book, the fracturing of the left-wing bloc has, for the most part, been the product of the European question. This problem has surged to prominence because of the link between EU membership and neo-liberal reforms: while one part of the old left-wing bloc was ready to embrace a rupture with the EU in order to stop these reforms, the other considered the pursuit of the integration process as its priority, even at the cost of institutional changes it did not support.

We find the same kind of fracture within Jean-Luc Mélenchon's own electorate – indeed, particularly sharply among voters who declare themselves close to France Insoumise.[66] Among this latter group, 52 per cent consider France's EU membership 'mostly a good thing' and 48 per cent 'mostly a bad thing'. It is thus obvious that the question of which aspiration to prioritize – the European Union or the social model – is central to the left's future. It is also self-evident that France Insoumise would have a lot to lose from a complete restruc-turing of the political landscape built on the divide between Europe

---

66   Among Mélenchon's voters in the presidential election, 64 per cent thought French EU membership was 'mostly a good thing', and 36 per cent that it was 'mostly a bad thing'.

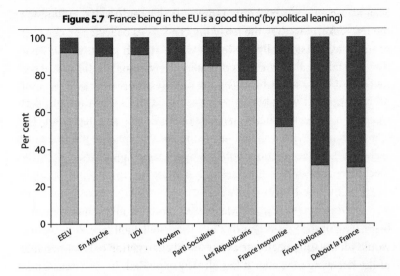

Figure 5.7 'France being in the EU is a good thing' (by political leaning)

and the nation – especially since the other parties' bases are highly homogenous on these questions.[67] The large majority of voters close to the Front National and Debout la France have a negative opinion of the European project, while those who say they are close to the other parties take an almost unanimously positive view.

Based on its 2017 electorate, France Insoumise seems to have taken a strategic decision framed in the following terms.[68] The first option would have been to define itself as a 'patriotic' movement that aimed to unite the whole of the popular classes, beyond the left–right divide, in what could be called a 'popular bloc'. This attempt would of course have taken place on bases very different to the Front National's own. But the difficulties associated with this option were the same as those faced by the FN: the expectations of low-income groups regarding so-called 'social' issues (security, immigration), as on economic policy and even on certain neoliberal reforms, were deeply contradictory and probably irreconcilable. The other possibility would be to work openly for a compromise on the left between a fraction of the popular classes

---

67   Ifop, *Ce que veulent les Français.*

68   For an analysis of Mélenchon's results and France Insoumise's strategic prospects, see Stefano Palombarini, 'Entre bloc bourgeois et stratégies d'opposition. Partie ouverte', *Contretemps* 35 (November 2017); and 'Quel compromis social pour une politique économique de gauche?', *Savoir/Agir* 42 (December 2017).

and a fraction of the bourgeois classes, challenging Macron's monopoly on the political representation of the latter.

The advantage of this second strategy is that it is consistent with the social base that Mélenchon really did assemble at the 2017 elections. But this cannot be a strategy turned towards the past, seeking to rebuild a left-wing bloc whose deep fracture is the result of thirty years of neoliberal policies associated with European integration. The contradictions within the old left-wing bloc on this last point are just as big as the contradictions within a hypothetical popular bloc – as the decline of the governmental left demonstrates.

But France Insoumise's real strategy probably transcends this opposition between an improbable 'people's bloc' and the likewise improbable recomposition of the traditional left-wing bloc. It is necessary to take seriously the political recomposition shown by the rise of the bourgeois bloc and Macron's victory – and to conceive a genuine renewal of political blocs rather than set out to reactivate unchangeable social groups following boundaries already defined in advance. The transformations of French capitalism have changed social structures and economic policy expectations; Macron's 'reforms' will pursue and accelerate this shift. This new situation must be the basis for any political strategy. The expansion of France Insoumise's electorate, if its ambition is indeed to reach power, must proceed by way of a defence of the peculiarities of a socioeconomic model rooted in the principles of solidarity and social justice – even without dreaming of an improbable unity of the popular classes on the basis of economic sovereigntism. Such a perspective would allow France Insoumise to mobilize a portion of abstainers and, most importantly, to aim to give political representation to fractions from other blocs doomed to be penalized by the transition towards a neoliberal model.[69] A central problem is how to prioritize their expectations. The strategy of seeking to constitute a genuinely renewed left-wing bloc – as opposed to one

---

69   There was 51 per cent abstention at the first round of the 2017 legislative elections. This figure had been 43 per cent in 2012, 40 per cent in 2007, 36 per cent in 2002, 32 per cent in 1997, and 31 per cent in 1993. We might note that the only time when the election was held based on proportional representation, in 1986, abstention had reached only 21 per cent. At the height of the left–right clash in 1978, it had been only 17 per cent.

reconstituted just as before – can only succeed if economic, environmental and social expectations become the front-rank concerns of a sufficient fraction of social groups, rather than those others habitually but inappropriately called concerns over 'culture' and social mores.

THE BOURGEOIS BLOC: A POLITICAL PROJECT WITH AN UNCERTAIN FUTURE

As we know, the images constructed and projected by the dominant media may respond to a logic totally at odds with any serious analysis of reality. In the case of Emmanuel Macron, this phenomenon has reached dizzying heights. The new president has proved to be the exact opposite of the image so insistently provided by his many partisans in the newspapers and on TV, who present him as a figure external to petty political games and blessed with great competence on economic matters. Macron's almost caricatural vision of the economy remains very much the view that a business banker would take. Everything can be reduced to a question of profit margins, and the answers to these questions take the form of mergers, acquisitions and the redeployment of assets. The possibility that tax measures favouring business will not encourage investment in production or innovation, resulting only in an inflation of financial assets, seems not to have crossed the mind of anyone in the government camp. It is telling, indeed, that anyone would unhesitatingly embrace measures that will push inequalities up yet further, at a moment when even organizations like the OECD and the IMF are troubled by the consequences of rising inequality. The criterion that guides the president's actions is not so much economic effectiveness as profit yields for finance. On the other hand, Macron has shown a genuine ability to strategize politically, determinedly and clear-sightedly occupying the space of the bourgeois bloc. This is a space that France's political crisis had left open for many years, but that no one before him had been able to identify and represent effectively.[70] The institutional reforms driven by the new government should thus be understood as the expression of a political project. Macron's action

---

70   See in particular Bruno Amable, Elvire Guillaud and Stefano Palombarini, *L'Éco-nomie politique du néolibéralisme. Le cas de la France et de l'Italie* (Paris: Éditions Rue d'Ulm, 2012).

should be analysed at the directly political level – on the basis of the concrete impact it will have on social conflict and its regulation.

THE BOURGEOIS BLOC, TRIUMPHANT BUT NOT (YET) DOMINANT

In such a perspective, the first point that needs to be underlined is the narrowness of the social base that lifted Macron to power in 2017. He was only apparently 'easily elected'.[71] It is true that his score in the second round (43 per cent of registered voters) was close to that of François Mitterrand in 1988 or Nicolas Sarkozy in 2007. But the fact that this was a face-off against a candidate from the Front National makes such comparisons inappropriate. The only precedent similar to the circumstances of Macron's election dates from 2002, when Jacques Chirac faced Jean-Marie Le Pen, and won much more massive support, with 62 per cent of registered voters. In the first round, Macron was chosen by 18 per cent of registered voters; among all ultimate winners, only Chirac had done worse, in 1995 (securing 16 per cent, when he faced another candidate, Balladur, from his own party) and in 2002 (14 per cent), after a *cohabitation* in government with the PS, which was politically costly for all concerned.

The indications that the bourgeois bloc has a very limited span of support – for the moment, at least – are sharpened by the reasons given by the voters who opted for Macron in the first round in 2017. The vote based on outright support was significant among those Macron voters who said that they were sympathetic to LREM (at 77 per cent), who represent the core of the new social alliance. Yet, among all of Macron's voters, the vote based on outright support amounted to under 48 per cent of the total – as against 61 per cent among Le Pen's voters, 72 per cent for Fillon, 69 per cent for Mélenchon and 71 per cent for Hamon.[72] This would reduce the level of outright support for the president's project to under one-tenth of the overall electorate.

These data indicate that Macron won *by default*, as a consequence of the political crisis analysed in this book. That is, it was the fracturing

---

71   He took 24 per cent in the first round and 66 per cent in the second.

72   Cevipof, *Le choix des électeurs: par adhésion ou par défaut, L'enquête électorale française: comprendre 2017*, wave 12b (April 2017).

of the old social blocs that allowed the emergence of a bourgeois bloc even though it is a minority in French society. For now, in the absence of any dominant pact, it is too early to know whether the new president's strategy will produce a solution to the crisis, affirming the hegemony of the new alliance, rather than an intensification of social conflict and thus a deepening of the crisis. But we can already identify the factors likely to contribute to the success or failure of the president's political project.

AT THE HEART OF THE NEW ALLIANCE: NEOLIBERAL REFORMS AND DEEPENED EU INTEGRATION

Despite what the dominant media discourse says, we ought to stress how unimportant so-called 'social' issues are to Macron's political strategy. The actions of the Philippe government and its interior minister spectacularly contradict the image of a social bloc consolidating around the defence of an 'open' society. Once we recognize this, we have to reject the cliché of a president who conforms to a certain political-science vulgate that reduces the political space to twin economic and 'cultural' axes – thus presenting him as the avatar of a 'modern' left, liberal in economics and progressive in cultural matters. Indeed, it is possible that some traditional PS voters who chose Macron even in the first round did entertain such a fantasy. But, since that moment at least, the reality should have opened their eyes. We ought to remember the signal sent to the (both economically and 'culturally') most right-wing electorate by Macron's visit to Philippe de Villiers[73] in August 2016; but also, and most importantly, the repressive migration policy – what *Marianne* called a 'malicious' policy,[74] completely abandoning what Macron had said during the election campaign.

The essential expectations of the groups making up the core of the bourgeois bloc have only a distant relationship with the defence

---

73   A politician and entrepreneur in the culture industry (through the Puy du Fou theme park), Philippe de Villiers, embodies a very conservative Catholic and nationalist right.

74   Speranta Dumitru 'L'actuelle politique migratoire de Macron ne respecte pas le programme d'En Marche', *Marianne*, 17 January 2018.

of an open, tolerant and multicultural society. But they are directly connected to the pursuit of European integration and the continuation of neoliberal reforms. The measures taken since the beginning of Macron's term work in this direction: the reforms were begun speedily and in numerous directions at once, without sparking any mass social opposition (by spring 2018, that is). But the deepening of the European project is a more delicate problem. The new government is conscious of the Eurozone's structural flaws, thus motivating its search for 'solutions' that would also be acceptable to the German authorities.[75] These would include a strengthening of market control over budget policies and the management of public debt, establishing the obligation to enact 'reforms', or even conditionality on transfers between countries (transfers that could not, in any case, become permanent).

The difficulties of forming a coalition government after the German elections in autumn 2018 delayed the enactment of any plan to reform the Eurozone. This would, in any case, be difficult to achieve, given the divergence between French proposals and the position that still seems to prevail in Germany. Considering the road that needs to be travelled, it seems that we can rule out any deep reform of European institutions in the short term; and the compromise that will probably end up emerging in the longer term has a high risk of disappointing many French expectations. This poses a political problem for Macron, since the incoherence of the Eurozone is likely to make support for European integration – the central pillar of the new alliance – rather more fragile. The example of Italy, which after long years of austerity has passed from almost-unanimous pro-European opinion to majority rejection of European integration, should provide cause for concern among the architects of the bourgeois bloc. The Partito Democratico, which governed for over six years on the basis of a social bloc very similar to that which Macron is trying to build in France, saw its electoral support fall sharply at the March 2018 general election. The winners were instead the Eurosceptic Five Star Movement and a party sharply hostile to European integration, the Lega.

---

75 See the various works of Jean Pisani-Ferry, the economist whom Macron's team takes as their point of reference.

SHOCK REFORMS: THE REASONS FOR THEM, AND THE RISKS THEY POSE

LREM's crushing majority in the National Assembly thus conceals a double weakness: the bourgeois bloc that brought Macron to power is in the minority in society, and also rests on a fragile electoral base. This double weakness itself explains the haste with which the government has embarked on 'reforms' that – if they succeed – will impose the almost complete transition of French capitalism towards a neoliberal model. As we have noted, the 'shock reform' strategy quickly produced a partial transformation of the new government's social base. At the first round of the presidential election, Macron obtained the support of 43 per cent of voters sympathetic to the PS and 20 per cent of those who favour the EELV (Greens). But by the time of the legislative elections, as LREM stood for parliament, these numbers had fallen to 27 and 10 per cent, respectively, while its support from voters who term themselves sympathizers of Les Républicains rose from 9 to 18 per cent.[76] This relative rightward shift in the new government's social base does not mark any deep change in the profile of the bourgeois bloc. But it doubtless does explain the sidelining of the progressive cultural and social themes that had taken up a certain place in Macron's election campaign discourse (and to which the dominant analyses have wrongly ascribed a decisive role in the construction of the new social alliance).

However, if we want to understand the strategy Macron has chosen – the high-speed neoliberal reform – we need to look beyond these short-term, tactical considerations. The crucial point lies in the long-term effects of these reforms, for – as in many other countries, especially Britain – the success of the neoliberal transformation of an economy and a society also involves a deep change in its social structures. That is, if neoliberalism is to endure, it must create its own social base.

The weaknesses within the bourgeois bloc do not, therefore, automatically imply the failure of the political project that aims to consolidate such a bloc. The 'reforms' have the capacity to produce (eventually) a substantial change in the political composition and weight of the social classes, and indeed of their expectations. This might

---

76   Data from FES 2017.

produce an expansion of the space the bourgeois bloc commands. This is the reason why, counting also on the opposition's difficulties, Macron has decided to proceed with the reforms as quickly as possible. The institutional changes in the new government's programme imply the alignment of the French economy to a model in which manufacturing industry occupies a reduced place, accelerating the decline of the working class and thus weakening the social base of both the left and the Front National.[77] Conversely, the development of a service sector – especially in finance – should make it possible to increase the number of white-collar employees liable to swell the ranks of the bourgeois bloc. We also see that the only clearly identifiable choice relating to economic strategy in the early phases of Macron's presidency has consisted of trying to attract the financial industries that, after Brexit, will quit London for Paris.

Thus, the gradual Uberization of major sectors of the economy, the development of start-ups – or, more modestly, of small businesses and even sole traders – are all called upon to increase the numbers of the self-employed, whether their work is genuinely autonomous or, in reality, directed externally. Workers' expectations regarding the social-protection system or employment production would be profoundly changed by such a social and economic shift, in a direction that would make them stand in less contradiction to the interests of the bourgeois bloc. Similarly, in a world of work where the role of waged employment was reduced, privatizations could be perceived less as a threat than as the source of new opportunities in terms of economic activity and jobs. The bid to reduce the political weight of the groups excluded from the bourgeois bloc is also apparent in the move to shrink the public-sector workforce – with a fall in posts concentrated among less skilled jobs, and the end of the special statuses that today push certain categories of workers to demand that the peculiarities of French capitalism be maintained.

These considerations indicate that the effects of Macron's 'reforms', if they are indeed successfully imposed, will work in the direction of

---

77   Emmanuel Macron, at that time the secretary-general adjunct at the Élysée, seems to have played a significant role in the highly controversial 2014 sale of a strategic part (the energy wing) of Alstom to General Electric.

consolidating the bourgeois bloc. They must, however, be qualified by another consideration that points in the opposite direction. That is, the accelerated transition towards a neoliberal model will inevitably produce a rise in inequality, and thus a pauperization of a part of the middle classes whose support is essential for the bourgeois bloc's ability to assert its own dominance.

This bid to weaken the social expectations in the French model – from employment protection to social protection, income redistribution, and even measures to boost purchasing power – relies on success in pushing up job numbers. Such a rise in employment levels is not alone enough to produce the change in expectations functional to the bourgeois bloc's viability. But it is doubtless a necessary precondition. From this point of view, in 2018 the economic cycle played in Macron's favour, but there are still major question marks over the longer-term future. We might doubt that start-ups can effectively substitute for big industrial firms' role in job creation; moreover, the deindustrialization intrinsic to the transition towards the neoliberal model poses a problem for the stability of France's trade balance, which risks further weakening France relative to Northern European countries (whose foreign trade balances are largely in surplus) in European negotiations that already look complex – and that, as we have said, are decisive for the viability of Macron's project.

The new regime's stability is thus linked to its capacity to aggregate a sufficient segment of the middle classes to a hard core made up of their richest members. The 'reforms' work in two directions that are – from this point of view – opposed. In the long term, they may produce a change in the social structure and in political demand that will make it easier to consolidate the bourgeois bloc. But other effects – both immediate and longer-term – will tend to shrink the new government's social base, which, need we remind ourselves, is very much in the minority already. This discrepancy between the political effects of these 'reforms' implies that the first phase of Macron's presidency will be decisive for the overall viability of his project. The new government is aware of this, and has thus decided to enact 'reforms' at marching speed.

FOR A NEW POLITICAL STRATEGY FOR THE LEFT

With Macron's election, the French crisis has entered a new phase, expanding the political conflict to encompass the entire institutional architecture. The overall organization of French capitalism is now at stake. We can easily grasp the dangers of a configuration in which the bloc in power excludes the popular classes as a whole, especially since the political and social opposition seems to have been weakened by the strategic problems to which we have referred. At the same time, the new social alliance is *already* far from dominant – that is, strong and coherent enough to ensure the viability of the strategy that seeks to consolidate this same alliance. Beating Macron is possible, then; and the bourgeois bloc may finally prove to be an illusion.[78] But that depends on the ability of an opposition concerned to defend the principles of solidarity and social justice to set itself a clear and effective strategy.

From this point of view, it is doubtless indispensable that the left re-centre the political debate on economic, environmental and social questions. Issues of 'identity' have burst onto the scene because of the efforts of the former parties of government. In converting to neoliberalism, these parties converged on an economic policy 'with no alternatives'; the functional need to differentiate among the political supply thus brought previously secondary questions into the foreground. But today, questions of 'identity' can serve as a way out for an opposition that lacks any economic or institutional strategy. This is particularly the case for the Front National and Les Républicains; indeed, we can predict that their programmes will tend to converge, on the basis of securitarian themes and questions linked to immigration and French identity. The opposition that wants to combat the complete transition of French capitalism towards a neoliberal model must set out to do the opposite: 'identitarian' themes must be side-lined, and the question of economic solidarity placed at the heart of political conflict.

Equally, the restructuring of the political landscape around an opposition between 'Europeanists' and 'patriots' would be a barrier

---

78   *Vaincre Macron* is the title of an interesting book by Bernard Friot (Paris: Éditions La Dispute, 2017).

to the construction of a real opposition to the bourgeois bloc. If the bourgeois classes may unite around the new government's economic and institutional project, the left–right cleavage is destined to divide the working classes for a long time to come, since they express profoundly contradictory expectations. The protection of disadvantaged groups – whose neglect produced the collapse of the Parti Socialiste – must be central to the progressive opposition's strategy. But a retreat onto the terrain of social solidarity in order to try to unite the whole of the popular classes, or indeed to try to build 'rotten compromises'[79] to win back the bourgeois classes seduced by Macron, would be a grave error with respect to the need to build an effective opposition to the bourgeois bloc. Reasserting, against the dominant discourse, the relevance of the left–right divide, implies giving up on two objectives: that of uniting the entire popular classes, and that of seeking to rebuild the identity of the 'old' left-wing bloc. We need to equip ourselves with the means to fight Macron as what he is: not the defender of an 'open society' opposed to cultural conservatism, or a convinced Europeanist who fights nationalism in all its forms, but, quite simply, a right-wing neoliberal president.

---

79   This literal translation of the German *Fauler Kompromiss* was used by Oskar Lafontaine in a 2009 speech at the Parti de Gauche's founding congress, with reference to the 'rotten compromises' the social-democratic parties had made.

Afterword to the English Edition

The election of Emmanuel Macron to the presidency of the Republic in 2017, followed by the absolute majority obtained by his movement La République en Marche (LREM) in the legislative elections, marked the electoral victory of a social bloc that is a minority – the bourgeois bloc. Without waiting, the new government launched a series of neo-liberal structural reforms, a preliminary analysis of which is offered in Chapter 5. These measures were followed by the pension reform, which had already been announced during the presidential campaign as the most significant of the five-year term, in the form of a bill that was brought to parliament for discussion at the beginning of 2020.

To summarize this reform briefly, we can say that it will transform a defined benefit system into a defined contribution system, lead to a general decrease in the level of public pensions, and facilitate the development of funded pensions and pension funds. The reform project has met with opposition from a majority of the population and aroused a social movement of considerable magnitude.[1] In the face of this social protest, the government has made only tactical withdrawals while persisting in its substantive approach, counting on its absolute majority in the National Assembly to overcome this opposition. Confident of its power, it has even forgone seeking the support of so-called 'reformist' trade unions, thus reaffirming its willingness to neglect all intermediate bodies in its general 'reform' project.

It is hardly surprising that the radical transformation programme implemented in 2017 has aroused substantial social opposition. However, the earliest sign of this opposition was not a response to the major reforms of social protection or labour legislation, but followed the announcement of a seemingly innocuous measure: a rise in fuel

---

1   At the end of 2019 and the beginning of 2020, all polls indicated that only a minority of French people approved of the reform project. The only group to show majority approval were the over-sixty-fives.

tax. Measures of this kind can, of course, serve as a spark for a social explosion in the making. That is what happened with the announcement of this tax increase, which, though presented as a measure to combat environmental degradation, was mainly motivated by the desire to offset the fall in tax revenue caused by the abolition of the wealth tax and the introduction of a flat tax on capital gains. Here we see the full ambiguity of the initial protest: was it opposition to the tax, which would make the *gilets jaunes* analogous to the 'Tea Party' in the United States, or a rejection of inequality?[2] The continuation of the *gilets jaunes* movement, which began in November 2018 and is still under way at the time of writing, has answered this question. The suspension of the tax increase and the emergency budgetary measures announced at the start of 2019 failed to extinguish a protest that has shifted to concerns that go far beyond those relating to the price of diesel (public services, democracy, and so on).

Both the tax policy and the 'structural reforms' undertaken by the Macron regime tend to increase inequalities in income and status. These effects are sometimes interpreted as the unfortunate but inevitable consequences of a 'modernization' of the economy in the era of globalization, which will disappear in the long term, once the new growth regime has set in. Beyond the dubious economic relevance of this reading of the transformations under way, it is useful to make a political reading of them. Rising inequalities and segmentation contribute to the break-up of old social blocs and favour, at least to some degree, the emergence of a new bloc that aspires to domination. We have explained in detail how the rupture of the traditional blocs of both right and left was necessary for the formation of a bourgeois bloc. This implies a breaking up of the perceived solidarities or communities of interest that underlay the existence of traditional blocs, particularly between certain sections of the middle and working classes.

But, despite being indispensable to the existence of the bourgeois bloc, this rise in inequalities in a large number of fields risks undermining the bloc itself, by weakening sections of the social groups it seeks to

---

2   In a publication at the end of 2019, the French statistical institute, INSEE, documented the rise in inequality and poverty rates due to the first fiscal measures taken by the government following the 2017 elections. INSEE Analyses 49, October 2019.

attract. A section of the middle classes may well be negatively affected by reforms that reduce public pensions, increase private healthcare costs, raise the cost of higher education, and so on. The stability of the new dominant social bloc is accordingly linked to its capacity to aggregate a sufficient fraction of the middle classes into a hard core made up of the most favoured groups. The 'structural reforms' thus have two opposite effects. They allow for a recomposition of social alliances that facilitates the emergence of the bourgeois bloc, but they are also likely to lead to a weakening of social groups peripheral to this bloc.

The social protest against the particular measures decided by the Macron regime (such as the pension reform, and the crises in schools, universities and hospitals), along with the *gilets jaunes* movement, illustrates these socioeconomic fractures. The visible sociology of the *gilets jaunes* is itself revealing of the new sociopolitical divide: the *gilets jaunes* are mostly people from the working classes or 'lower' middle classes; their demands are essentially focused on material conditions of existence (purchasing power, access to public services, and so on). This movement, like others (the railway workers' movement against reform of their industry, the movement against education reform and in defence of the public sector, the doctors' protest in public hospitals), has placed socioeconomic issues and, to put it in the simplest possible terms, the conflict between capital and labour at the centre of political conflict.

Macron thus found himself faced with a major political difficulty. At the heart of his project is the complete restructuring of French institutional architecture in a direction totally favourable to capital; but a political confrontation organized around the conflict between capital and labour would see the bourgeois bloc in great difficulty, as its perimeter would be reduced, and support for the government weakened.

To overcome this contradiction, Macron's strategy developed on three different levels. The first, as we pointed out, relied on a very rapid reform process, which the government hoped, assuming its success, would profoundly shift the constellation of interests and the social balance of power. We saw a very clear example of this in the law reforming the pension system, for which the government did not hesitate to resort to Article 49–3 of the Constitution, allowing the law to be approved without a vote in parliament. It should be stressed that there was no doubt that the law would be approved, given the strong and compact presidential majority in the National Assembly; if Macron decided to use this extraordinary procedure, it was simply to save time. And time is a precious resource for a government with an urgent need to delegitimize the unions, and signal just as quickly to the workers that their future depends on the profitability of capital. In this sense, a pension reform drawn up without any real negotiation with the trade unions, even those more amenable to a compromise, linking the level of pensions to the rate of growth and beginning the transition to a capitalization system, is a very strong signal to the world of labour: if you oppose capital, your future will be threatened. In this way, a reform process implemented in the absence of majority support would reduce the political weight of the interests of labour, making possible a consolidation of the bourgeois bloc once the transition to the neoliberal model was complete.

The second level of Macron's strategy, necessary to overcome the difficulties of a project entirely focused on defending the interests of capital, and for this reason backed for the moment only by a social minority, bears on the definition of the cleavages that structure the political conflict. Clearly, it is in the president's interest to reactivate confrontations that are relatively disconnected from economic issues, which would both divide social opposition and divert attention from the conflict between capital and labour. In February 2020, while the law on pensions was being debated in the National Assembly, President Macron and his government thus launched a major media offensive against the 'Islamic separatism' that supposedly threatens the unity of the Republic.

It is worth recalling that a strategy of the same type had characterized the action of the Valls government when François Hollande was president, which was strongly challenged over its economic reforms, particularly those concerning employment law. But this strategy had not prevented the collapse of the Socialist government, its only effect being to facilitate the presence of Marine Le Pen in the second round of the presidential election. One may ask what political rationality leads to an almost identical recapitulation of a strategy that had proved to be a loser as recently as 2017. To gain a perspective on this, it is useful to widen our gaze beyond France's borders, where we see that, wherever the neoliberal model asserts itself, political struggle is structured around two poles that oppose (or pretend to oppose) each other on themes such as immigration, secularism and national identity, while converging on the direct and complete subjection of public policy to the interests of capital. This explains why Macron saw Marine Le Pen as his favourite opponent: not just because he considered it would be easier to beat her in a second round that would allow him once again to play the role of defender of the Republic, but also because a possible victory for Le Pen would not call into question the essence of the economic reforms he had promoted. Returning to the pension reform, we have accordingly seen the Rassemblement National (former Front National) 'oppose' it without once being present on a picket line, without taking part in or organizing the slightest demonstration, and practically without taking the floor in the parliamentary debate.

The third level of Macron's strategy – the most brutal and visible – is police repression of the opposition movement. Protests against the labour law under the Hollande presidency had already been suppressed by the police and gendarmerie with extreme brutality, characterized by the use of new 'policing' techniques such as 'kettling' and an abandonment of what was previously considered the traditional French policy of avoiding contact with demonstrators as far as possible. Police violence had already reached a new level in the repression of protest movements linked to the defence of the environment.[3] But with the *gilets jaunes* movement, police repression took on another dimension. From December 2018, the Macron government's tactic was to repress the *gilets jaunes* brutally, using as a pretext the material damage committed in Paris by some demonstrators during its second weekend action. The brutal attitude of the police was subsequently confirmed, even – or perhaps especially – towards nonviolent demonstrators. The government used all the possibilities at its disposal: preventive arrests, banning of demonstrations, premature interruption of marches

---

3   A demonstrator against the Sivens dam, Rémi Fraisse, was killed in October 2014 following a grenade attack by a gendarme.

which had nevertheless been authorized, and so on. The results of this repression indicate the extraordinary nature of the repressive action: between December 2018 and February 2020, twenty-five people lost an eye as a result of stun grenades, five had a hand severed, and more than 900 cases of filmed police violence were tallied by journalist David Dufresne. Amnesty International has denounced this shocking repression on several occasions.[4]

This strategy is easily explained in terms of the factors analysed above. Macron's government rests on a relatively narrow social base compared to the traditional social blocs of left and right. After the tidal wave of the 2017 legislative elections, the institutions of the Fifth Republic give him full latitude to push through reforms without significant opposition. The dominant media (press, television and radio) are largely owned by oligarchs who support Macron's socioeconomic project. The only potentially significant opposition is on the street; and police repression makes it possible to contain this, or even significantly weaken it. This tactic has its risks, especially in terms of image, but also its advantages. By appearing to represent the party of order, Macron can hope to broaden his social base to more traditionally conservative social groups.

The repressive tactic can thus serve the strategy of permanent socioeconomic transformation, which requires a stabilization of the bourgeois bloc as the dominant group. We can return to the three abstract models of capitalism presented in the preface and envisage a hybridizing, however awkward, of these models as social bases. A hybridizing of the respective neoliberal and 'illiberal' models is not a utopia. It might even ultimately appear the most 'natural' path of neoliberal transformation, given the opposition that 'structural reforms' are likely to provoke. Failing to convince a majority, the neoliberal model can impose itself by defeating its opponents, not only at the ballot box but also in the street. The neoliberal transition phase would then facilitate this political hybridization, which could eventually

---

4 We could add the death of Zineb Redouane on the sidelines of a *gilets jaunes* demonstration in Marseille in December 2018, or that of Steve Maia Caniço in Nantes in June 2019.

become obsolete, once the neoliberal transformation was complete.[5]

We may conclude more generally that the transition to the neo-liberal model always poses problems of the same type: a social bloc capable of supporting this model only consolidates itself *after* the reforms have been completed. The Thatcher transition was uncertain in its beginnings; it was accompanied by brutal repression (the miners' strike of 1984) and favoured by external events (the Falklands War). Similarly, in Italy, the transition to the neoliberal model in the first half of the 1990s was facilitated by the delegitimizing of the entire political class following the *mani pulite* investigations and the action of the so-called 'technical' governments that took over.

It is difficult, at the time of writing, to predict whether Macron's strategy will prove successful. However, a few points are already certain. It is clear that the analysis we presented in 2017, before Macron's accession to power, was well-founded: the social bloc he sought to con-solidate is indeed a bourgeois bloc, from which the working classes are excluded. The project of a bourgeois bloc represents an attempt to respond to the political crisis marked by the fracture of traditional social alliances, both left and right, while preserving the interests of socially privileged groups. It should be remembered, however, that when this book was first published, two months before the 2017 presidential elections, Macron presented himself, was complacently presented by the dominant media, and was even widely perceived by the population, as a progressive modernizer, attentive to social and minority rights, and still ambiguous about the verticality of power[6] – a president who would open the political debate to civil society and allow the spread of social democracy at all levels. Three years on, not much remains of this image. Macron is certainly a 'modernizer', but in a very precise sense: all his action is aimed at the rapid and complete transition of French capitalism to the neoliberal model.

In this, as we have pointed out, Macron's action is in continuity

---

5   If ever the Rassemblement National came to power, which is not impossible, there is little doubt that France would continue on the same neoliberal trajectory of police repression.

6   A verticality that he would 'accept' one year after his election. 'Macron "totally" accepts the "verticality" of presidential power', *Le Figaro*, Le Scan Politique, 27 April 2018.

with that of the governments that preceded his presidency over the last thirty-five years. There is, however, a discontinuity involved in Macron's election, since his reforms – which complement those on finance and currency, privatizations, and the markets for goods and services – tackle the most socially sensitive institutional areas, such as social protection, labour relations (thus complementing Hollande's 'work') and pensions. Such a modernization of French capitalism is hardly compatible with a government basing its action on a social bloc that includes, even if only in a peripheral position, sections of the working classes: this explains both the crisis of the traditional blocs and the emergence of the bourgeois bloc. If Macron is a modernizer, he must therefore rely on rapid and uncompromising decision-making, and cannot afford to waste time either in negotiations with social partners or in debates in parliament. The authoritarian exercise of power and the violent repression of social protest are not problems that Macron might correct, but, for the reasons we have given, con-stituent elements of his political project. The Macron who may run for president in 2022 will be the same as the Macron who won in 2017; but this time, no one will be able to say they were deceived about his programme, his social reference points or his conception of power.

March 2020